index

This recipe is really just an excuse to eat lots of fresh strawberries and cream. Don't feel pressured to make a "perfect" meringue. This is supposed to be messy and something you want to eat, not something you are afraid to touch! It doesn't matter if the meringue splits or isn't crispy; it's not meant to be.

strawberry meringue roulade

Preheat the oven to 250°F.

Put the egg whites in a grease-free bowl, add the cornstarch and beat until soft peaks form. Add 1 tablespoon of the superfine sugar at a time, beating well between each addition, and continue beating until you can no longer feel grains of sugar when you rub the mixture between your thumb and forefinger. Use a large metal spoon to transfer the mixture to the prepared baking sheet and smooth it out with a palette knife. You want a rectangle about 8 x 12 inches and no thicker than ½ inch.

Bake the meringue in the preheated oven for 20 minutes, until it is just set and the top turns a light caramel color and is no longer sticky when lightly touched.

Take a second piece of baking parchment, slightly larger than the meringue, and sprinkle over 1 teaspoon of superfine sugar. Quickly flip the tray upside-down so that the meringue is turned out onto the paper. Tap the bottom of the baking sheet so that the meringue comes away in one piece. Peel off the bottom piece of baking parchment. Firmly roll the meringue up into a log with the second sheet of paper and wrap in a clean kitchen towel. Set aside to cool completely.

Put the cream and confectioners' sugar in a bowl and whisk until firm peaks form. Unroll the meringue. Spoon the cream over the meringue, leaving a 1-inch margin around the edge. Arrange the strawberries over the cream and roll up. Dust with confectioners' sugar and cut into thick slices to serve.

3 egg whites

1 teaspoon cornstarch

¾ cup superfine sugar, plus 2 teaspoons

½ cup whipping cream

3 tablespoons confectioners' sugar, plus extra for dusting

2 cups strawberries, hulled and sliced

a baking sheet, lined with baking parchment and sprinkled with 1 teaspoon superfine sugar

serves 4—6

cinnamon, spice, & warm apple pie

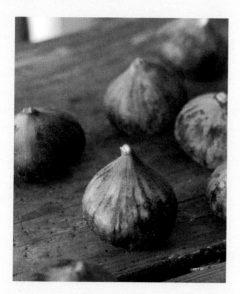

Don't be tempted to use large figs here, as they will split and prevent the egg whites from cooking and the meringue will become sloppy. Instead look out for small, very black ones as they will work perfectly with the caramelly, golden meringue.

fresh fig & walnut meringue

1 cup walnut halves

8–10 small black fresh figs, halved

6 large egg whites

1¼ cups light soft brown sugar

a circle of baking parchment, 8 inches diameter

serves 8–10

Preheat the oven to 350°F.

Put the walnuts on a baking sheet and toast in the preheated oven for 5 minutes, until just starting to turn golden. Remove and let cool. Do not turn off the oven.

Put the egg whites in a large, grease-free bowl and beat until they form soft peaks. Add one tablespoon of the sugar at a time, beating well between each addition, and continue until all the sugar has been added and the meringue is thick and fluffy and a caramel color. Add the figs and walnuts and stir to combine.

Put the circle of baking parchment on a baking sheet. Use a large spoon to transfer the mixture onto the paper, keeping within the circle and using the back of the spoon to create dents and peaks.

Bake in the preheated oven for 40–45 minutes, until the peaks of the meringue are dark golden. Slide a large knife under the meringue to remove it from the paper and transfer it to a serving plate. Serve warm.

There is a lovely retro charm, redolent of 1950s cookbooks, about making a sweet cake with a vegetable that's usually served savory. Of course, the zucchini here performs the same function as grated carrot does in the more familiar carrot cake. It keeps this cake wonderfully fresh and moist.

lemon, zucchini, & poppyseed cake

Preheat the oven to 375°F.

Put the poppyseeds and grated lemon peel in a small bowl. Heat the milk until hot, stir it into the poppyseed mixture, and let it cool while you make the cake mixture.

Cream the butter and sugar together until very light and fluffy. Beat in the egg yolks, one at a time, followed by the vanilla extract, flour, and ground almonds. Fold in the zucchini, followed by the poppyseed mixture. In a separate, grease-free bowl, whisk the eggs whites with the cream of tartar until stiff, then fold the egg whites into the cake mixture. Scrape the mixture into the prepared pan and level the surface.

Bake in the preheated oven for 50–60 minutes, until just firm to the touch and a skewer inserted into the center comes out clean. Let the cake cool in the pan for 10 minutes before turning out onto a wire rack.

When cool, sift the confectioners' sugar into a bowl, make a well in the center and add the still-hot melted butter. Start to mix, adding sufficient lemon juice to make a spreadable frosting. Mix in the grated lemon peel, then spread over the cake. Leave for 1–2 hours to set before serving.

3 tablespoons poppyseeds

finely grated peel of 2 lemons

⅓ cup milk

2 sticks unsalted butter, softened

1⅛ cups light soft brown sugar

4 large eggs, separated

½ teaspoon vanilla extract

1½ cups self-rising flour, sifted

⅔ cup ground almonds

9 oz. zucchini, topped, tailed, and coarsely grated

½ teaspoon cream of tartar

for the frosting:

1 cup confectioners' sugar

2 tablespoons unsalted butter, melted

1 teaspoon finely grated lemon peel

2–3 tablespoons freshly squeezed lemon juice

a springform cake pan, 9 inches diameter, buttered and baselined

serves 8–10

cinnamon, spice, & warm apple pie

comforting baked fruit desserts for chilly days

RYLAND
PETERS
& SMALL
LONDON NEW YORK

Senior Designer Iona Hoyle
Commissioning Editor Julia Charles
Production Toby Marshall
Art Director Leslie Harrington
Publishing Director Alison Starling

Indexer Hilary Bird

First published in the United States
in 2010
by Ryland Peters & Small
519 Broadway, 5th Floor
New York, NY 10012
www.rylandpeters.com

10 9 8 7 6 5 4 3 2 1

Text © Fiona Beckett, Tessa Bramley,
Maxine Clark, Ross Dobson, Tonia George,
Brian Glover, Caroline Marson, Laura
Washburn, and Ryland Peters & Small
2010

Design and photographs
© Ryland Peters & Small 2010

Printed in China

  Library of Congress Cataloging-in-
Publication Data
Cinnamon, spice & warm apple pie :
comforting baked fruit desserts for chilly
days.
    p. cm.
  Includes index.
  ISBN 978-1-84975-054-7
  1. Baking. 2. Desserts. 3. Cookery
(Fruit)
  TX763.C497 2010
  641.6'4--dc22

2010021274

Notes

• All spoon measurements are level
unless otherwise specified.

• Eggs are large unless otherwise
specified. Free-range eggs are
recommended. Uncooked or partly
cooked eggs should not be served to
the very young, the very old, those with
compromised immune systems, or to
pregnant women.

• When a recipe calls for the grated peel
of lemons or limes, buy unwaxed fruit and
wash well before using. If you can only find
treated fruit, scrub well in warm, soapy
water before using.

• Ovens should be preheated to the
specified temperature. Recipes in this
book were tested using a regular oven.
If using a fan-assisted oven, follow the
manufacturer's instructions for adjusting
temperatures.

contents

introduction

What could be more enticing and take the edge off of a cold winter's day than an apple crumble warm from the oven or a blackberry cobbler, bubbling up with rich juices? Simple, delicious, and cherished—these old-fashioned fruit desserts are experiencing a long overdue revival. In this collection of recipes you'll find all of your best-loved desserts in one place. Whether you are searching for the perfect ending to a dinner party or a treat to wrap up any night of the week, these quick and easy-to-prepare ideas will soon become firm favorites.

The old-time fruit desserts here have long been called by various names but what they have in common is that they are all homey recipes based on seasonal fruits that rely more on good fresh ingredients than fancy preparation. A crumble is the classic British comfort food—fruit sprinkled with a melt-in-mouth pastry crumb mix. Betties are a classic American baked pudding made of alternate layers of sugared fruit and buttered breadcrumbs—a recipe created to make use of stale leftovers. Another iconic recipe is the cobbler, which is basically stewed fruit on top of which a biscuit dough is dropped in lumps before baking. (It is said that the dish got its name as the cooked dough resembles cobblestones.) A clafoutis is a French dessert that comprises fresh fruit baked in a rich egg custard. The wonderfully descriptive slump is also a battered dessert but unlike clafoutis is most often cooked, or at least started, on top of the stovetop in a baking pan rather than in the oven. Recipes for crisps are open to interpretation but they are often a simple fruit bake topped with crumbled cookies or pastry and baked. The curiously named pandowdy is an upside-down fruit pie with a rolled crust top, which is broken up with a spoon. Also included are great recipes for other popular fruit-based bakes such as pies, tarts, and strudels, as well as some deliciously moist fork cakes.

There is nothing like a homebaked fruit dessert, so create a little nostalgia in your kitchen with one of these classic recipes.

crumbles &
streusels

There is no better partner for apples than ripe, juicy blackberries. This easy dessert is simply divine served warm from the oven with a scoop of vanilla ice cream. If there's any leftover, have it with Greek-style yogurt for breakfast.

apple & blackberry crumble

Preheat the oven to 400°F.

Put the apples, blackberries, and sugar in a bowl and use your hands to mix well. Transfer to the prepared baking dish.

To prepare the crumble topping, combine the oats, flour, sugar, almonds, and cinnamon in a bowl and mix well. Add the butter. Using your fingertips, rub in the butter until the mixture resembles coarse bread crumbs. Alternatively, use a food processor and blend carefully with the pulse button but do not over-process or you will grind the oats too finely.

Sprinkle the crumble topping evenly over the apple mixture. Bake in the preheated oven for 35–45 minutes, until the crumble is golden and the fruit is bubbling. Serve warm with vanilla ice cream.

2 lbs. mixed apple varieties, peeled, cored, and chopped

1 lb. blackberries

¼ cup sugar

vanilla ice cream, to serve

for the crumble topping:

1 cup porridge oats

1 cup all-purpose flour

½ cup light soft brown sugar

½ cup ground almonds

½ teaspoon ground cinnamon

1 stick plus 2 tablespoons unsalted butter, chilled and cubed

a medium ovenproof dish or 4–6 individual dishes, well buttered

serves 4–6

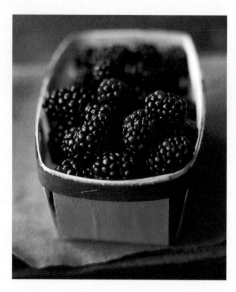

Fresh berries are so tasty and good just as they are that it's tempting not to fuss with them too much. That said, they are also very good used in a crumble. The floral aroma of blackberries can be enhanced by adding a small splash of rosewater or orange blossom essence to the berries. Keep this in mind whenever you are serving or cooking with any red berry.

blackberry crumble

12 oz. blackberries

1 tablespoon sugar

1 teaspoon cornstarch

for the crumble topping:

1 cup all-purpose flour

5 tablespoons unsalted butter, chilled and cubed

¼ cup light soft brown sugar

chilled cream, to serve

a medium ovenproof dish, lightly buttered

serves 4

Preheat the oven to 350°F.

Put the blackberries in a bowl with the sugar and the cornstarch and toss to mix. Tumble the berries into the prepared baking dish and set aside for 15–20 minutes.

Put the flour and butter in a bowl and, using your fingertips, rub the butter into the flour until the mixture resembles coarse bread crumbs. Stir in the brown sugar.

Sprinkle the crumble mixture evenly over the berries and bake in the preheated oven for 45–50 minutes, until the top is golden brown. Let the crumble cool slightly before serving with cream.

Plums have such a rich flavor when they are cooked that they need little or no other flavorings with them, except perhaps a pinch of cinnamon. You could also bake this recipe with yellow plums, greengages, or mirabelles—they will all be delicious. For a special treat, toss the uncooked plums in a little damson or sloe gin.

simple plum crumble

Preheat the oven to 350°F and put a baking sheet on the middle shelf to heat.

Halve the plums and remove the pits. Cut the halves into quarters if they are very large. Toss them with the sugar and tip them into the prepared baking dish.

To make the crumble topping, use your fingertips to rub the butter into the flour with the salt until it resembles coarse bread crumbs. Alternatively do this in a food processor. Stir in the sugar.

Lightly scatter the crumble topping over the plums. Place the baking dish on the hot baking sheet and bake in the preheated oven for 40–45 minutes, until golden brown.

Remove from the oven and serve warm with cream.

8–10 ripe plums

4–5 tablespoons sugar

chilled cream, to serve

for the crumble topping:

½ stick plus 1 tablespoon unsalted butter, chilled and cubed

1⅓ cups all-purpose flour

a pinch of salt

¼ cup sugar

a medium ovenproof dish, butttered

serves 4–6

This luscious crumble is sophisticated enough for a smart dinner party. Chocolate and pears were made for each other—here the chocolate melts and mixes with the pear juice to make a delicious sauce. Pumpernickel makes an interestingly crunchy topping, and gives the dessert a dramatic look.

pear & chocolate crumble

2–3 large not-too-ripe pears

¼ cup sugar

2–3 tablespoons drinking chocolate (not unsweetened cocoa) or grated dark chocolate

finely grated zest of ½ a lemon

chocolate ice cream or chilled cream, to serve

for the pumpernickel topping:

4 oz. sliced pumpernickel

4 oz. stale brown bread

4 tablespoons drinking chocolate (not unsweetened cocoa) or grated dark chocolate

½ stick unsalted butter, chilled and cubed

⅓ cup demerara sugar

a medium ovenproof dish, buttered

serves 4

Preheat the oven to 350°F and put a baking sheet on the middle shelf to heat.

Peel, core, and slice the pears and put them in the prepared baking dish so that they fill it by two thirds. Sprinkle the sugar, drinking chocolate, and lemon zest over the top and mix well to coat the pears. Cover and set aside.

To make the crumble topping, tear up the pumpernickel and bread slices and put in the bowl of a food processor. Pulse for a minute or so until very roughly crumbed. Add the drinking chocolate, butter, and sugar and pulse again for a minute or so until finer crumbs form. Do not over-process or it will form a solid lump.

Uncover the pears and sprinkle lightly and evenly with the topping mixture. Place the baking dish on the hot baking sheet and bake in the preheated oven for 25–30 minutes, until the pears are very tender and the topping is crisp.

Remove from the oven and serve warm with chocolate ice cream or cream.

Gooseberries seem to have a natural affinity with ginger. Ginger wine is a delicious tipple on its own but it really brings out the flavor of gooseberries. It's best to cook the fruit a little first to draw out the juice (as it makes the crumble too wet and sloppy) but you can reserve this liquid, warm it and serve alongside the cooked crumble.

gooseberry & ginger crumble

Preheat the oven to 375°F and put a baking sheet on the middle shelf to heat.

Put the gooseberries in a non-reactive saucepan, add the ginger wine and sugar and cook gently until the fruit starts to burst. Remove from the heat and tip the gooseberries into a strainer set over a clean saucepan to catch the juices. Put the gooseberries into the prepared baking dish, covering the base with a single layer. Reserve the juices for later.

To make the ginger topping, put the flour, ginger, salt, and butter in the bowl of a food processor and process until it resembles coarse bread crumbs. (Alternatively you can rub in by hand.) Tip into a mixing bowl and stir in the sugar.

Lightly sprinkle the topping evenly over the gooseberry mixture, mounding it up a little towards the center. Place the baking dish on the hot baking sheet and bake in the preheated oven for about 25 minutes, until crisp and golden.

Remove from the oven and let cool for 5 minutes before serving with the warmed reserved juices and clotted cream.

2 lbs. gooseberries, topped and tailed

3 tablespoons ginger wine

½ cup sugar

clotted cream, to serve

for the ginger topping:

1½ cups all-purpose flour

1 teaspoon ground ginger

a pinch of salt

1 stick unsalted butter, chilled and cubed

½ cup sugar

a medium ovenproof dish or 4 individual dishes, well buttered

serves 4

Crumbles are normally considered to be a comforting winter pudding, but this deliciously light, nutty version makes the most of juicy summer nectarines. It takes very little time to prepare and tastes sublime with ice cream.

nectarine & pistachio crumble

6 nectarines

vanilla ice cream, to serve

for the nutty crumble topping:

½ cup shelled pistachios, coarsely chopped

⅓ cup blanched whole almonds

½ cup oat flour or oatmeal ground in a food processor

½ stick unsalted butter, chilled and cubed

½ cup all-purpose flour

¼ cup light soft brown sugar

a baking sheet lined with baking parchment

serves 6

Preheat the oven to 425°F.

To make the crumble topping, put the pistachios and almonds in a food processor and process until coarsely chopped. Transfer to a bowl. Add the oatmeal and butter and use your fingertips to rub the ingredients together until the mixture resembles coarse, wet sand. Add the flour and sugar and rub together to combine. Cover and refrigerate until needed.

Cut the nectarines in half. If the pit does not come out easily, don't worry—simply slice the flesh off the fruit and drop it directly onto the prepared baking sheet. Sprinkle the crumble topping evenly over the nectarines and bake in the preheated oven for 10–15 minutes, until the fruit is soft and juicy and the topping is a soft golden color. Serve warm with ice cream.

The holiday season is definitely coming when the smell of this crumble starts to drift around the house. A classic mixture of dried fruits provides a rich base for the light crumble topping. The spicy mulled wine seeps into the fruits as they cook and plumps them up nicely.

mulled mixed fruit crumble

Preheat the oven to 375°F and put a baking sheet on the middle shelf to heat.

Chop the dried fruits into bite-size pieces and place in a nonreactive saucepan. Add the wine, mulling spices, orange peel, and sugar. Heat gently, then let simmer for 10 minutes. Set aside to cool.

Spoon the semi-cooked dried fruit into a baking dish and remove the mulling spices and orange peel.

To make the topping, put the flour, mixed spice, salt, and butter into a food processor and process until it looks like coarse bread crumbs. (Alternatively you can rub in by hand.) Tip the mixture into a bowl and stir in the sugar.

Lightly sprinkle the topping mixture evenly over the surface of the dried fruits, mounding it up a little towards the center. Place on the hot baking sheet and bake in the preheated oven for about 25 minutes, until crisp and golden on top.

Remove from the oven and let cool for 5 minutes before serving with cream.

12 oz. mixed dried fruits (such as golden raisins, apples, apricots, figs, and cranberries)

1 generous cup red wine

1 small cheesecloth bag of mulling spices for wine (cinnamon, cloves, and allspice)

a strip of orange peel

¼ cup sugar

heavy cream, to serve

for the spiced crumble topping:

1½ cups whole-wheat flour

¼ teaspoon ground mixed spice

a pinch of salt

1 stick unsalted butter, chilled and cubed

½ cup demerera sugar

a medium ovenproof dish

serves 4

Rhubarb holds vivid childhood memories for most people. Whether it's of dipping young raw rhubarb sticks into sugar and munching away or enjoying a delicious crumble with plenty of cream. Orange seems to draw out and temper the sharp flavor of rhubarb with delicious results.

rhubarb & orange crumble

1½ lbs. forced rhubarb

2 large oranges

a pinch of ground ginger

¾ cup light soft brown sugar

heavy cream, to serve

for the almond topping:

1 cup all-purpose flour

a pinch of salt

⅔ cup ground almonds

1 stick unsalted butter, chilled and cubed

1 cup blanched almonds, chopped

¼ cup demerara sugar

a medium ovenproof dish

serves 4

Preheat the oven to 400°F and put a baking sheet on the middle shelf to heat.

Trim the rhubarb, cut it into large chunks and put it in a large saucepan. Finely grate the peel from the oranges and add to the rhubarb. Stir in the ginger and sugar and cook over a gentle heat for a few minutes, stirring occasionally until the rhubarb begins to release its juices but is still holding its shape. Pour the rhubarb into a strainer set over a bowl to catch the juices and reserve these for later. Remove the pith from the oranges with a small sharp knife then cut out the segments between the membrane. Add to the drained rhubarb and set aside to cool completely.

To make the almond topping, put the flour, salt, ground almonds, and butter into a food processor and process until it looks like coarse bread crumbs. (Alternatively you can rub in by hand.) Tip the mixture into a bowl and stir in the chopped nuts and sugar.

Spoon the rhubarb and oranges into a baking dish. Lightly sprinkle the almond topping evenly over the surface, mounding it up a little towards the center. Place the baking dish on the hot baking sheet and bake in the preheated oven for about 35 minutes, until crisp and golden.

Remove from the oven and let cool for 5 minutes before serving with the warmed reserved juices and cream.

Pine nuts and almonds, with their toasty flavors, add another dimension to this simple crumble. The crust is quite loose so it will need to settle before it crisps up, which is perfect because crumble is best eaten warm rather than piping hot. The brown sugar thickens the plum juices to create a caramel which bubbles up to stain the nutty crust.

nutty plum crumble

Preheat the oven to 350°F.

Halve and pit the plums and arrange them in a single layer in a baking dish. Add the orange peel and juice. Sprinkle over 2 tablespoons of the sugar and dot over 2 tablespoons of the butter. Cover with foil and bake in the preheated oven for about 25–30 minutes, until the plums are beginning to soften.

Put the flour, ground almonds, and the remaining butter in a bowl and rub it between your fingertips until it forms lumps. Stir in the flaked almonds, pine nuts, and the remaining sugar.

Remove the baking dish from the oven, discard the foil, and scatter over the crumble topping. Return to the oven and bake for about 30 minutes, until the topping is golden and the juices are bubbling through. Let sit for 10 minutes to allow the crust to firm up. Serve with cream.

12 ripe plums

2–3 thick strips of peel and the freshly squeezed juice from 1 orange

⅓ cup light soft brown sugar

1 stick unsalted butter, chilled and cubed

¾ cup self-rising flour

⅓ cup ground almonds

3 tablespoons slivered almonds

3 tablespoons pine nuts

chilled cream, to serve

a medium ovenproof dish

serves 4

These little crumbles are a bit of a fiddle to make, but well worth the effort. Be very careful when transferring them from the pan to the plate—a trusty fish slice will help. They make an impressive dinner party dessert and a rather more sophisticated alternative to banoffi pie.

toffee banana crumbles

8 firm bananas

¼ cup light soft brown sugar

freshly squeezed juice of 1 lemon

chilled heavy cream or sour cream, to serve

for the coconut topping:

⅓ cup all-purpose flour

⅔ cup unsweetened dried shredded coconut

½ stick unsalted butter, chilled and cubed

2 tablespoons sugar

a cast-iron skillet
4 individual heatproof chef's rings
(each about 3-inches diameter)

serves 4

Preheat the oven to 375°F.

Trim and cut the bananas into 1¼-inch lengths. Reserve four of the lengths for the centers of the crumbles, then slice each of the remaining ones in half lengthwise. Sprinkle the brown sugar into a skillet, then place the chef's rings into the sugar. Pack each ring with an upright banana. Next, tightly surround this with the split bananas (to resemble the petals of a flower) and pour the lemon juice over the top.

To make the topping, put the flour, coconut, and butter in a food processor and process until it resembles coarse bread crumbs. (Alternatively you can rub in by hand.) Tip into a bowl and stir in the sugar.

Fill each ring to the top with the coconut topping. Transfer the skillet to the preheated oven and bake for about 25 minutes, until the crumbles are golden. Remove from the oven and slip a fish slice under each ring to lift them out of the pan and onto warmed serving plates.

Carefully remove the rings and serve with the pan juices spooned around the crumbles and cream.

This crumble is based on a famous Scottish dessert, combining raspberries with toasted oatmeal, whiskey, heather honey, and cream. If you are using frozen raspberries, there is no need to defrost them first. The oat topping packs a satisfyingly toasty crunch.

cranachan crumble

Preheat the oven to 375°F. Put a baking sheet on the middle shelf to heat.

Put the raspberries in a baking dish. Drizzle with about 3 tablespoons of the honey and pour in the cream and whiskey.

To make the topping, melt the butter and the remaining honey in a saucepan and stir in both types of oats. Stir until they start to clump together like a crunchy breakfast cereal.

Sprinkle the oat mixture evenly over the surface of the raspberries, mounding it up a little towards the center.

Place the baking dish on the baking sheet in the preheated oven and bake the crumble for about 20–25 minutes, until crisp and golden on top.

Let cool for 5 minutes before serving with cream.

12 oz. fresh or frozen raspberries

6 tablespoons heather honey

½ cup heavy cream

2 tablespoons whiskey

lightly whipped heavy cream, to serve

for the oatmeal topping:

¾ stick unsalted butter

¾ cup fine oatmeal

1 cup rolled oats (not instant)

a medium ovenproof dish

serves 4–6

This delicious streusel is really nice made in individual dishes or cups, but make sure they are ovenproof. Serve each guest their own little pitcher of cold cream so that they don't feel greedy reaching over the table for more!

cranberry & orange streusel

1 lb. fresh or frozen cranberries

finely grated peel and freshly squeezed juice of 1 orange

honey, to taste

chilled light cream, to serve

for the streusel topping:

½ cup all-purpose flour

⅓ cup light soft brown sugar

¾ stick unsalted butter, chilled and cubed

a medium ovenproof dish

serves 4

Preheat the oven to 425°F.

Put the cranberries in a saucepan with the orange juice and bring to a boil. Cook for 2 minutes then remove from the heat and sweeten to taste with honey. Pour into a baking dish and let cool.

Mix the flour, sugar, and grated orange peel in a bowl and add the butter. Rub the butter into the dry mixture until it resembles fine bread crumbs and is on no account greasy or oily. (Pop into a plastic bag and leave in the fridge for 20 minutes if it has become so.)

Once the cranberries are cold, sprinkle the topping evenly over the top. Bake in the preheated oven for 10 minutes, then reduce the oven temperature to 350°F and bake for a further 15 minutes.

Remove from the oven and serve warm with cream.

Here the halved pears act as an edible dish. It is really important to caramelize the cut side of the pears to a dark mahogany to bring out their flavor. Don't add too much egg to the almond mix—it must be quite lumpy so that it doesn't flow out of the pears as it cooks.

bourbon pears with frangipane streusel

Preheat the oven to 375°F.

Halve the pears, and scoop out the cores. Melt the sugar in a heavy skillet and cook until a good dark caramel. Splash in the bourbon, then add the pears cut-side down with the butter. Cook over medium heat for 10 minutes or until the cut side of the pears turns a rich dark brown. Remove from the heat and arrange the pears cut-side up in a baking dish. Pour the cooking juices around the pears.

To make the frangipane topping, mix the ground almonds, chopped almonds, and sugar with a splash of bourbon and enough beaten egg until it begins to clump together. Mound this mixture on top of the baked pears and scatter with the slivered almonds. Bake in the preheated oven for 20–25 minutes, until golden.

Remove from the oven, spoon over the caramelized juices, and serve warm with whipped cream or vanilla ice cream.

2 large pears

¼ cup sugar

¼ cup bourbon

1 stick less 1 tablespoon unsalted butter

vanilla ice cream or whipped cream, to serve

for the frangipane topping:

1 cup ground almonds

⅓ cup chopped or nibbed almonds

⅔ cup sugar

an extra splash of bourbon

1 egg, beaten

½ cup slivered almonds

a medium ovenproof dish

serves 4

cobblers & more

Cranberries add a pleasing tang to this cobbler. If you can't easily find fresh cranberries, simply buy dried ones and soak them for at least one hour in warmed cranberry juice before using.

cranberry & apple cobbler

Preheat the oven to 425°F.

Pick over the cranberries and wash them. Peel and core the apples, then slice them thickly. Put all but 1 cup of the cranberries and the apples into a saucepan with the orange peel and juice and the cloves. Poach gently for about 15—20 minutes, until the fruit is juicy and tender. Set aside and let cool.

Roughly chop the remaining cranberries. Rub the butter into the flour and salt until it resembles fine bread crumbs. Stir in the sugar and chopped cranberries. Add the milk, mixing with a blunt knife to form a fairly soft, sticky dough. Tip the dough out onto a floured work surface and roll out to a thickness of about ¾ inch. Stamp out rounds with a cookie cutter.

Spoon the fruit into a baking dish and arrange the rounds against the edge of the dish, overlapping them slightly and leaving a gap in the center. Brush the top of the rounds with milk. Bake in the preheated oven for 10—15 minutes, until the pastry is golden brown. Serve hot with cream.

1 lb. fresh or frozen cranberries or ½ cup dried cranberries

1 lb. cooking apples

finely grated peel and freshly squeezed juice of 1 small orange

a pinch of ground cloves

chilled heavy cream, to serve

for the cobbler topping:

½ stick unsalted butter, chilled and cubed

1¾ cups self-rising flour

a pinch of salt

¼ cup sugar

about ⅔ cup milk, plus extra to glaze

a medium ovenproof dish
a fluted 1½—2 inch cookie or biscuit cutter

serves 4

This style of cobbler is quite similar to a French clafoutis but the batter uses more flour and has baking powder instead of eggs to lift it. Use big juicy blackberries for this recipe and the batter will be marbled with their color.

blackberry cobbler

1¾ all-purpose flour

¼ teaspoon mixed spice (optional)

⅔ cup sugar

a large pinch of salt

4 teaspoons baking powder

1 cup milk

½ teaspoon vanilla extract

½ stick unsalted butter

1½ lbs. fresh or frozen blackberries

chilled cream or hot custard, to serve

a large metal baking pan

serves 4–6

Preheat the oven to 350°F.

Sift the flour, mixed spice (if using) sugar, salt, and baking powder into a bowl. Gradually whisk in the milk and vanilla extract to give a thick batter. Let sit for 15 minutes.

Melt the butter over a gentle heat in a shallow, metal baking pan. Give the rested batter a quick stir, then pour the batter into the pan over the melted butter. Don't worry if the butter floats around and mingles with the batter at this stage.

Immediately scatter the blackberries over the batter and transfer the cobbler to the preheated oven. Bake for about 55 minutes, until the batter has puffed up and set.

Serve warm with cream or custard.

This American classic should be eaten soon after baking because the cobbler dough soaks up the fruit juices upon standing, but that doesn't mean you should overlook any leftovers as a breakfast option the next day!

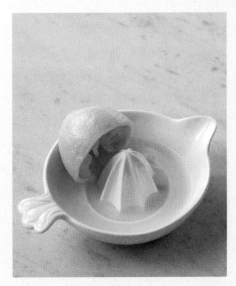

peach cobbler

Preheat the oven to 375°F.

Cut the peaches in half, remove the pits, then cut each half into 3 slices. Arrange the slices in a baking dish, sprinkle with the flour, and toss well to coat evenly. Add the lemon juice and honey and stir. Set aside.

To make the topping, put the cream and crème fraîche in a large bowl and stir well. Put the flour, sugar, baking powder, baking soda, and salt in a separate bowl and mix well. Add the butter and rub in with your fingertips until the mixture resembles coarse bread crumbs. Using a fork, stir in the cream mixture until blended—use your hands at the end if necessary, the mixture should be sticky, thick, and not willing to blend easily.

Drop spoonfuls of the mixture on top of the peaches, leaving gaps to expose the fruit. Sprinkle sugar liberally over the top. Bake in the preheated oven for 25–35 minutes, until golden.

Serve warm with cream or vanilla ice cream.

6 not-too-ripe peaches

1 tablespoon all-purpose flour

1 tablespoon freshly squeezed lemon juice

3 tablespoons honey

chilled cream or vanilla ice cream, to serve

for the cobbler topping:

½ cup heavy cream

5 tablespoons crème fraîche or sour cream

1¼ cups all-purpose flour

¼ cup sugar, plus extra for sprinkling

1 teaspoon baking powder

¼ teaspoon baking soda

a pinch of salt

4 tablespoons unsalted butter, chilled and cut into pieces

2–3 tablespoons sugar, for sprinkling

a large ovenproof dish

serves 6

This easy recipe is just as good made with raspberries, blackberries, or blueberries. For a light scone topping, use your hands to shape the dough (a rolling pin is too heavy for such a light mixture.) The walnuts and brown sugar become pleasingly crisp and contrast well with the airy scones.

raspberry & apple crispy cobbler

5 red eating apples

1 lb. raspberries

1 tablespoon sugar

whipped cream, to serve

for the cobbler topping:

2 cups self-rising flour

½ teaspoon salt

3 teaspoon baking powder

1 tablespoon sugar

4 tablespoons unsalted butter, chilled and cubed

⅓ cup milk mixed with ⅓ cup water

1 egg

1 tablespoon light cream

2 tablespoons coarsely chopped walnut pieces

1 tablespoon brown sugar

confectioners' sugar, for dusting

a medium ovenproof dish
a 2-inch fluted cookie or biscuit cutter

serves 4–6

Preheat the oven to 425°F.

Peel, core, and thinly slice the apples. Put the apples and raspberries in a baking dish, sprinkle with the sugar and toss gently to coat the fruit in sugar.

To make the topping, sift the flour, salt, and baking powder into a bowl, then stir in the sugar. Rub in the butter with your fingertips until the mixture resembles fine bread crumbs.

Put the milk and water mixture in a separate bowl. Add the egg and beat well. Make a well in the flour mixture, then pour in the egg mixture. Using a palette knife, draw the mixture lightly together to form a soft dough.

Turn the dough out onto a floured work surface and quickly and lightly knead the dough until smooth. Form into a ball with the sides of your hand and press out evenly and lightly with the flat of your hand to a thickness of about ½ inch. Stamp out 8 rounds with a cookie cutter, then arrange them down the sides or around the edge of the baking dish (depending on the shape of your dish), on top of the fruit, leaving a space in the center so they will cook evenly. Brush with the cream and sprinkle with the walnuts and brown sugar.

Bake in the preheated oven for 5 minutes. Reduce the oven temperature to 400°F and bake for a further 20 minutes, until the scones are well risen, golden brown, and crisp with a light, fluffy center. Dust with confectioners' sugar and serve with whipped cream.

Dark bubbling blueberries hide under a light cobbled crust of lemony polenta cake. The secret of this dish is not to spoon the blobs of topping mixture too close together—leaving a little space around each one allows the fruit to bubble up through the gaps.

blueberry & lemon cobbler

Preheat oven to 350°F.

Spread the blueberries out in a baking dish. Cream the stick of butter with the sugar and grated lemon peel, until pale and fluffy. Beat in the sour cream. Sift the flour with the polenta, baking powder, and salt and fold into the cream mixture. Dot small spoonfuls of the mixture over the blueberries in a very random manner, until the top of the dish has been covered, leaving about 1 inch space around each one. (This will give the dish its "cobbled" look, and the juices from the fruit will bubble up around the dough.) Bake in the preheated oven for about 20 minutes, until the top is firm. While the cobbler is baking, prepare the butter mixture for the crust.

Put the remaining butter in a small saucepan with the honey, lemon juice, and sugar and melt over low heat. Remove the cobbler from the oven and pour this mixture over the crust.

Increase the oven temperature to 375°F. Return the cobbler to the oven and cook for a further 15–20 minutes, until golden. Serve warm with vanilla ice cream.

1½ lbs. blueberries

1 stick plus 1 tablespoon unsalted butter, at room temperature

⅓ cup sugar

finely grated peel and freshly squeezed juice of 1 lemon

½ cup sour cream

½ cup all-purpose flour

½ cup fine polenta

3 teaspoons baking powder

½ teaspoon salt

2 tablespoons honey

¼ cup sugar

vanilla ice cream, to serve

a medium ovenproof dish, buttered

serves 4

These cheeky little desserts will raise a smile as you bring them to the table. Use deep ramekins to achieve the impressive starry effect. They look truly spectacular and taste just as good as they look!

pear, maple, & pecan cobblers

4 small ripe pears

finely grated peel and freshly squeezed juice of ½ a lemon

4 tablespoons pure maple syrup

for the cobbler topping:

½ stick unsalted butter, chilled and cubed

1¾ cups self-rising flour

a pinch of salt

3 tablespoons maple syrup

1 scant cup milk

½ cup roughly chopped pecans

heavy cream or Greek-style yogurt, to serve

a 1½ –2 inch cookie or biscuit cutter
4 individual ovenproof ramekins
or similar

serves 4

Preheat the oven to 425°F.

Peel and core the pears, then slice them thickly lengthwise. Put them in a saucepan with the grated lemon peel and juice and the maple syrup. Poach gently for 10 minutes until the fruit is almost tender. Set aside.

To make the topping, use your fingertips to rub the butter into the flour and salt until it resembles fine bread crumbs. Stir the maple syrup into the milk and add ⅔ cup only of this mixture to the flour, mixing with a blunt knife to form a fairly soft, sticky dough. Tip the dough out onto a floured work surface and roll out to a thickness of about ¾ inch. Stamp out rounds with a cookie cutter.

Arrange the pear slices around the edge of the ramekins like a star, with the thicker ends in the center of the dish and the thinner ends pointing upwards out of the dishes. Spoon the juice evenly over the pears and anchor them with a round of cobbler dough placed lightly in the center (the pears should poke out all around the dough). Brush the top of the cobblers with the remaining milk and sprinkle with the chopped pecans. Carefully transfer the ramekins to a baking sheet and bake in the preheated oven for 10–15 minutes, until the dough is puffed and golden brown, and the pears just browning at their tips. Serve hot with cream or Greek-style yogurt.

A truly decadent dessert for cold winter days. The sugar melts into the cream around the bananas, making a rich and sticky sauce. Cutting the topping into little rounds helps it to cook faster and looks very decorative. You could try making other shapes—such as hearts or flowers—using a variety of cookie cutters.

molasses banana cobbler

Preheat the oven to 425°F.

Peel the bananas and slice thickly. Arrange in a baking dish. Mix the cream with the brown sugar and pour this mixture over the bananas.

Sift the flour and salt into a bowl and rub in the butter. Stir in the sugar and cinnamon. Combine the molasses and milk, whisking with a fork until the molasses has dissolved. Quickly pour the treacle mixture into the flour mixture and mix to form a soft dough. Tip the dough out onto a floured work surface and knead briefly until smooth. Use the flat of your hand to pat out to a thickness of ¾ inch. Stamp out as many rounds as you can with a cookie cutter, re-rolling the trimmings as necessary. Use these to cover the bananas.

Brush with a little milk and bake in the preheated oven for 15–20 minutes, until the scones are well-risen and golden brown on top. Cover with a piece of foil if the scones are cooking too quickly and the banana is still raw.

Serve warm with cream or vanilla ice cream.

4 medium bananas

⅔ cup heavy cream or canned evaporated milk

2 tablespoons dark soft brown sugar

chilled cream or vanilla ice cream, to serve

for the molasses scone topping:

1¾ cups self-rising flour

a pinch of salt

½ stick unsalted butter, chilled and cubed

2 tablespoons sugar

½ teaspoon ground cinnamon

3 tablespoons dark molasses

⅔ cup milk, plus extra for glazing

a 1¼-inch cookie or biscuit cutter
a medium ovenproof dish

serves 4

Rosewater add a delicate flavor to these pretty individual cobblers. Freezing the raspberries first makes it easier to set them into the dough but keep half unfrozen to pile on top of the cobblers for decoration.

little raspberry & rose cobblers

1¼ lbs. raspberries, half of them frozen

petals from 2 pink or red roses, washed and dried (optional)

½ stick unsalted butter, chilled and cubed

1¾ cups self-rising flour

a pinch of salt

¼ cup sugar

about ⅔ cup milk

1 tablespoon rosewater extract

confectioners' sugar, for dusting

chilled cream, to serve

a 4-cup, nonstick muffin pan or 4 individual silicone muffin cups or similar

serves 4

Preheat the oven to 425°F.

Select the most attractive rose petals and put these to one side to use as decoration. Shred the remaining ones. Use your fingertips to rub the butter into the flour and salt until it resembles fine bread crumbs. Stir in the sugar and shredded rose petals.

Combine the milk and rosewater extract and pour into the flour mixture, mixing with a palette knife to form a fairly soft and sticky dough. Tip out onto a floured work surface and roll out to a thickness of about ½ inch. Stamp out 4 rounds that will fill the cups in your muffin pan.

Place the rounds gently in the pan and carefully push the frozen raspberries into the dough. Dust with confectioners' sugar and bake in the preheted oven for 10–15 minutes, until the dough is risen and golden brown. Let the cobblers cool in the pan for a few minutes before carefully lifting out. Serve warm with the remaining raspberries, a scattering of rose petals, a dusting of confectioners' sugar, and some cream for pouring.

This deliciouly fruity cobbler is covered with tiny lemon-flavored dumplings. You can use whatever berries are available but frozen mixed red berries are convenient and work very well.

berry cobbler

Preheat the oven to 400°F.

Pick over the berries, discarding any really soft or bruised fruits. Mix them with the crème de cassis (if using) and sugar and transfer to a baking dish.

Rub the butter into the flour and salt until it resembles fine bread crumbs. Stir in two thirds of the sugar and the grated lemon peel. Add the milk to the flour mixture, stirring with a blunt knife to form a fairly soft and sticky dough. Tip the dough out onto a floured work surface and knead lightly. Roll into a long thin sausage and using scissors, snip off little hazelnut-size pieces. Scatter these lightly over the berries.

Mix the lemon juice with the remaining sugar and liberally brush this mixture all over the dumplings. Bake in the preheated oven for 15 minutes, until the scones are golden brown and the fruit bubbling. Serve hot with cream.

2 lbs. mixed red berries (raspberries, blueberries, strawberries, blackberries, black currants, cherries, etc)

3 tablespoons crème de cassis (optional)

3 tablespoons sugar

chilled light cream, to serve

for the lemon cobbler topping:

½ stick unsalted butter, chilled and cubed

1¾ cups self-rising flour

a pinch of salt

⅓ cup sugar

finely grated peel of 2 lemons and freshly squeezed juice of 1 lemon

scant ¼ cup milk

a medium ovenproof dish

serves 4—6

A pandowdy is made with a sweet dough baked on top of fruit, the crust being "dowdied" by pushing it into the wonderfully fruity juices to soften it before serving. It can also be served upside down like a tarte tatin (see page 117).

plum & hazelnut pandowdy

2 lbs. plums

½ cup light soft brown sugar

½ teaspoon ground cinnamon

finely grated peel and freshly squeezed juice of 1 small orange

3 tablespoons unsalted butter, chilled and cubed

chilled cream, to serve

for the pandowdy crust:

2 cups all-purpose flour

3 tablespoons sugar

1 tablespoon baking powder

1 stick less 1 tablespoon unsalted butter, chilled and cubed

2½ oz. finely ground hazelnuts

generous ⅔ cup light cream

sugar, for dusting

a cast-iron skillet or heavy baking pan (about 10–11 inches diameter)

serves 6

Preheat the oven to 425°F.

Halve the plums and slice them thickly. Put them in a bowl and add the sugar, cinnamon, grated orange peel, and juice. Stir to combine then tip the plums into a cast-iron skillet. Dot with the cubes of butter. Set aside.

To make the pandowdy crust, sift the flour, sugar and baking powder into a mixing bowl. Use your fingertips to rub the butter into the flour until the mixture resembles coarse bread crumbs. Mix in the ground hazelnuts. Stir in all but a couple of tablespoons of the cream with a palette knife, until the mixture comes together to form a sticky dough. Tip the dough out onto a floured work surface and knead very lightly until smooth.

Working quickly, roll the dough out to a circle ¼ inch thick and ½ inch wider than the skillet. With the help of the rolling pin, lift the dough over the fruit and over the edge of the pan. (Do not press the crust onto the sides of the pan.) Make a couple of slits in the dough to allow steam to escape. Brush with the remaining cream and dust with sugar.

Put the pan on a baking sheet to catch any leaking juices and bake in the preheated oven for 10 minutes, then reduce the oven temperature to 350°F and loosely cover with foil. Return the pandowdy to the oven and bake for a further 35–40 minutes, until the crust is golden.

Remove from the oven and "dowdy" the crust by sharply pushing it under the surface of bubbling fruit with a large spoon. Serve warm with cream.

This is a traditional pudding from the British West Country—little known, but highly deserving of a larger audience. It is simplicity itself to make using a food processor and uses basic ingredients.

apple dappy

Put the apples in a saucepan with the lemon juice, sugar, and butter and cook, uncovered, over medium heat until softened. Remove from the heat and set aside.

Preheat the oven to 425°F.

In the bowl of a food processor, combine the flour, baking powder, baking soda, and salt and pulse a few times to blend. Add the butter and sugar and pulse until the mixture resembles fine bread crumbs. Leave the motor on and add the cream and half of the milk. The dough should be soft and sticky. If it is too stiff, add the remaining milk.

Transfer the dough to a floured work surface. You need to roll it out to a 8 x 12 inches rectangle and it should be almost exactly that, not more.

Spread the cooled apple mixture over the dough and roll up from a long end, as you would a jelly roll. Mark 7 equal pieces on the roll, then cut into slices using a sharp knife. Arrange the slices, cut-side-up in the prepared baking pan, with one in the center and the others around it. (They should not actually touch as the dough will expand during baking.)

Sprinkle generously with sugar and bake in the preheated oven for 20–25 minutes, until puffed and golden. Let cool slightly and serve warm with cream.

1 lb. tart eating apples, such as Cox's or Braeburn, peeled, cored, and diced

freshly squeezed juice of ½ a lemon

2 tablespoons sugar

1 tablespoon unsalted butter

clotted or heavy cream, to serve

for the pastry:

1½ cups all-purpose flour

1 teaspoon baking powder

1 teaspoon baking soda

a pinch of salt

½ stick unsalted butter

2 tablespoons sugar

2 tablespoons clotted or heavy cream

½ cup milk

sugar, for sprinkling

a small square or circular baking pan, lined with baking parchment and lightly buttered

serves 7

bettys & crisps

If you have the patience, you can crack the apricot kernels and take out the nuts inside. These are very like bitter almonds, and are a fantastic addition when chopped and toasted with the bread crumbs.

buttered apricot betty

Preheat the oven to 375°F.

Halve the fresh apricots and remove the pits (or drain the canned apricots and pat dry.) Arrange a layer of apricots on the bottom on a baking dish.

Reserve 4–6 tablespoons of bread crumbs for the top. Sprinkle some of the rest of the bread crumbs over the apricots in the baking dish, and dot with some of the butter. Put in some more apricots and repeat these alternate layers until all the apricots and bread crumbs are used up. Use the reserved bread crumbs for the final top layer.

Warm the syrup with the orange juice, and pour this over the top. Sprinkle with sugar and dot with the remaining butter.

Place the baking dish in a roasting pan and pour in enough boiling water to come half way up the sides of the dish. Bake in the preheated oven for 45 minutes, until the apricots are soft and the top crisp and brown. Serve warm with cream.

1 lb. fresh apricots or 3 x 14-oz. cans apricots in juice (not syrup)

1 stick unsalted butter, cubed

3 cups fresh bread crumbs, lightly toasted

2 tablespoons corn or golden syrup

scant ½ cup fresh orange juice

¼ cup sugar

chilled cream, to serve

a medium deep pie or soufflé dish, buttered
a large roasting pan

serves 4

Pineapple, rum, and coconut—three flavors that are just made for each other. Blocks of sweetened coconut cream are perfect for grating into desserts, as you can use just the amount you like, and the rest keeps for ages in a plastic bag.

pineapple rum betty with coconut

1 medium pineapple

1 cup unsweetened dried shredded coconut

3 oz. vanilla pound cake or similar, crumbed

3-oz. piece of creamed coconut block, grated

¾ stick unsalted butter

4 oz. macadamia nuts, roughly chopped

2 tablespoons corn or golden syrup

½ cup dark or golden rum

chilled cream, to serve

a medium deep pie or soufflé dish, buttered

a large roasting pan

serves 6

Preheat the oven to 375°F.

Cut the top and bottom off the pineapple, then cut off the skin, removing the "eyes" using the tip of a potato peeler. Cut into quarters and then take out the hard core. Slice thinly.

Spread the shredded coconut evenly over a baking sheet and toast in the preheated oven for about 5 minutes, until pale golden brown. Mix with the crumbed cake and half of the grated creamed coconut.

Place a layer of the sliced pineapple in the prepared baking dish. Reserve 4–6 tablespoons of the toasted coconut mixture for the top. Sprinkle some of the rest of the coconut mix over the pineapple and dot with butter. Put in some more pineapple and repeat these alternate layers until all the pineapple and coconut are used up. Mix the reserved coconut with the chopped macadamia nuts and use this for the final top layer.

Warm the syrup with the rum, and pour this over the top. Sprinkle with the remaining grated creamed coconut and dot with the remaining butter. Place the pie dish in a roasting pan and pour in enough boiling water to come half way up the sides of the dish. Bake in the preheated oven for 35–40 minutes, until the pineapple is soft and the top crisp and brown. If the top browns too much, lay a piece of foil loosely on top. Serve warm with cream.

This is a traditional American recipe with very humble origins. It is often made with apples but not necessarily dried cranberries. Just like English bread pudding, it is an economic way to use up stale bread but it tastes even better if you use fresh white bread or even brioche.

apple betty with dried cranberries

Preheat the oven to 375°F.

Combine the apples, cinnamon, grated orange peel, apple juice and cranberries in a large bowl. Toss gently with your hands to mix and set aside.

In a separate bowl, combine the bread crumbs and melted butter and mix well. Spread about one-third of the buttered bread crumbs in the bottom of the prepared baking dish. Add the pecans and sugar to the remaining bread crumbs and mix to combine.

Put half of the apple mixture on top of the bread crumbs in the baking dish. Top with half the bread crumb and pecan mixture and top this with the remaining apple mixture. Finish with the remainder of the bread crumb and pecan mixture. Dot with the butter and bake in the preheated oven for 30–40 minutes, until golden and crisp. Serve warm with cream.

2 lbs. tart eating apples, such as Cox's or Granny Smith, peeled, cored, and diced

1 teaspoon ground cinnamon

1 tablespoon finely grated orange peel

⅓ cup fresh apple or orange juice

⅔ cup dried cranberries

3 cups white bread crumbs

⅜ stick unsalted butter, melted

⅔ cup chopped shelled pecans

½ cup light soft brown sugar

2 tablespoons unsalted butter, cut into pieces

whipped cream, to serve

a medium deep pie or soufflé dish, well buttered

a large roasting pan

serves 4–6

A cheat's way of making caramel is to melt caramel candies in butter, as this takes away all the worry of caramelizing sugar. Adding polenta or cornmeal to this crisp topping gives it a lovely crunch. It looks very homey baked in a heavy cast-iron skillet but an ordinary ovenproof dish is fine too.

caramel apple crisp

6 tart eating apples, such as Cox's or Granny Smith, peeled, cored, and diced

freshly squeezed juice of ½ a lemon

½ stick unsalted butter

4 oz. hard caramel candies, crushed or chopped

a pinch of ground cinnamon

chilled sour cream or vanilla ice cream, to serve

for the oat crisp topping:

½ cup fine polenta or cornmeal

¾ cup rolled oats (not instant)

¾ stick unsalted butter, melted

½ cup demerara sugar

a cast-iron skillet

serves 6

Preheat the oven to 375°F.

Core and thickly slice the apples and toss them with the lemon juice. Melt the butter in a heavy cast-iron skillet that will go in the oven, then add the crushed caramel candies. Stir until melted, add the apples and cinnamon and toss well to coat in the buttery caramel. Set aside.

To make the oat crisp topping, put the polenta, oats, and sugar in a bowl and mix well. Stir in the melted butter and work through the mixture with your fingertips until it resembles coarse bread crumbs.

Lightly sprinkle the topping mixture evenly over the surface of the apples, mounding it up a little towards the center. Bake in the preheated oven for 40 minutes, until browned and crisp. Serve warm with sour cream or vanilla ice cream.

This is a very useful recipe for when nectarines are slightly hard, as cooking them softens the flesh and brings out the flavor. Ginger goes particularly well with this fruit so ginger cookies are used here but if they are not available, simply substitute them with your favorite crunchy cookie and add a good pinch of ground ginger to the topping mixture.

nectarine & ginger crisp

Preheat the oven to 375°F. Put a baking sheet on the middle shelf to heat.

Halve the nectarines and remove the pits, then slice or chop them. Tip them into a baking dish and mix with the apple juice, chopped ginger, and sugar.

To make the ginger topping, melt the butter in a saucepan and stir in the crushed cookies and sugar until the mixture resembles coarse bread crumbs.

Lightly sprinkle the topping mixture evenly over the surface of the nectarines, mounding it up a little towards the center.

Place the baking dish on top of the hot baking sheet and bake in the preheated oven about 25 minutes, until crisp and golden on top. Serve warm with vanilla ice cream or cream.

6 medium nectarines

2 tablespoons finely chopped stem ginger

scant ⅛ cup fresh apple juice

¼ cup sugar

vanilla ice cream or chilled cream, to serve

for the ginger crisp topping:

1 stick unsalted butter, melted

7 oz. gingersnap cookies, crushed

½ cup demerera sugar

a medium ovenproof dish

serves 4

This is a back-to-front crumble. The crumble and mango are baked separately, then served together for maximum crunch. You can prepare the topping in bulk and store it in an airtight container so that you can make a really exotic dessert at a moment's notice. Do serve coconut ice cream with this, if you can find it.

mango & coconut macaroon crisp

2 ripe mangoes

finely grated zest and freshly squeezed juice of 1 lime

vanilla or coconut ice cream, to serve

for the coconut macaroon topping:

2 tablespoons whole-wheat flour

3 tablespoons unsalted butter

½ cup unsweetened dried shredded coconut

3 oz. coconut macaroon cookies

3 tablespoons demerara sugar

4 small, ovenproof dishes

serves 4

Preheat the oven to 400°F.

Peel the mangoes with a potato peeler. Slice the sides from the mangoes as near to the pit as possible, then slice or chop the flesh, including any still clinging to the stones. Toss this with the grated lime peel and juice and spoon into 4 individual baking dishes (these must be shallow, as the mango needs to go into something that heats through quite quickly). Put them on a baking sheet and cook in the preheated oven for about 15 minutes, while you make the topping.

To make the topping, rub the flour, butter, and coconut together until it resembles coarse bread crumbs. Lightly crush the macaroon cookies in a plastic bag, then stir these into the coconut mixture along with the sugar. Spread out onto a nonstick baking sheet and put in the oven with the mango. Toast the topping for 10–15 minutes, until crisp. Remove both sheets from the oven and sprinkle the toasted coconut macaroon topping over the hot mango.

Serve immediately with coconut or vanilla ice cream.

Some cooks like to remove the skins from the peaches before pitting them but keeping them on here will add color and texture to the finished dish. This can be made in individual shallow bowls or in one big dish, as you prefer. As it is quite buttery, it's best to serve it with any type of cream, except ice cream.

peach & amaretti crisp

Preheat the oven to 375°F. Put a baking sheet on the middle shelf to heat.

Cut the peaches in half, remove the pits, then cut the peach halves into quarters. Toss with the Amaretto liqueur, if using. Arrange the peaches in a baking dish, cut-side up and in a single layer.

Roughly crush the amaretti cookies in a plastic bag using a rolling pin. Mix the ginger syrup and egg yolk together and stir or lightly rub into the crushed cookies until the mixture looks quite lumpy and rough. Stir in the chopped ginger.

Scatter the mixture over the peaches and dot with butter. Transfer the dish to the hot baking sheet and bake in the preheated oven for 20–25 minutes, until the peaches are tender and the amaretti topping is brown and crisp. Serve warm with crème fraîche or sour cream.

4–6 large, firm but ripe peaches or nectarines

2 tablespoons Amaretto di Saronno liqueur or similar (optional)

chilled crème fraîche or sour cream, to serve

for the amaretti topping:

9 oz. amaretti (or ratafia) cookies

1 egg yolk

2 tablespoons finely chopped stem ginger plus 2 tablespoons of the syrup

¾ stick unsalted butter, chilled and cubed

a medium ovenproof dish

serves 4

There is a dessert in south-west France called Pastis Gascon, which is an apple or prune tart with a feather-light topping of sugar-dusted phyllo pastry, suffused with fiery Armagnac. This recipe re-interprets the traditional recipe and makes it into a type of fruit crisp.

apple, prune, & armagnac phyllo crisp

4 sheets phyllo pastry, thawed if frozen

1 stick unsalted butter, melted

4 eating apples

16 ready-to-eat pitted prunes

2–3 tablespoons Armagnac or Cognac

3 tablespoons sugar

finely grated peel of 1 lemon

confectioners' sugar, to dust

hot crème anglaise or chilled cream, to serve

a medium ovenproof dish

serves 4

Preheat the oven to 375°F.

Lay the phyllo out on a clean work surface and brush with the melted butter. Leave to set and dry out for 15–20 minutes.

Meanwhile, peel, core, and slice the apples and quarter the prunes. Toss them together in a bowl with the Armagnac, sugar, and the grated lemon peel. Pile the fruit into a baking dish, cover with foil, and bake in the preheated oven for 20 minutes.

Scrunch the pastry up so that it rips and tears and breaks into small rags. Remove the apple and prune mixture from the oven and lightly scatter the phyllo pieces on top, making sure it looks quite ragged and spiky. Return to the oven to bake for a further 20 minutes, until golden brown. Dust liberally with confectioners' sugar and serve warm with crème anglaise or cream.

clafoutis, slumps,
& puddings

Traditionally, this classic French dish is made using the first cherries of the season, but it is equally lovely with other orchard fruits such as small peaches, nectarines, or apricots. The best thing about this recipe is that the batter can be made the day before, refrigerated overnight then poured over the fruit and baked when you are ready for dessert.

cherry clafoutis

Preheat the oven to 425°F.

Spread the almonds out on a baking sheet and toast in the preheated oven for 6–8 minutes, until lightly golden. Let cool.

Put the cooled almonds in a food processor. Use the tip of a small sharp knife to scrape the seeds from the vanilla bean directly into the food processor. Process until the mixture resembles a coarse meal. Add the flour and sugar and process just to mix. Add the eggs, egg yolks, and cream and process again until you have a smooth, thick batter. Transfer to a bowl, cover, and refrigerate until needed.

Arrange the cherry halves in the bottom on a baking dish. Carefully pour the batter over the cherries. If need be, rearrange the cherries to evenly distribute.

Cook in the preheated oven for 25 minutes, until the clafoutis is puffed up and golden brown. Let cool for a few minutes before serving—the clafoutis will sink during this time. Serve hot with vanilla ice cream.

1 cup blanched almonds

1 vanilla bean, split lengthwise

3 tablespoons all-purpose flour

1¼ cups sugar

4 eggs

2 egg yolks

1 cup light cream

8 oz. cherries, halved and pitted

vanilla ice cream, to serve

a medium, shallow ovenproof dish

serves 4

This delicious dessert is ideal for entertaining because it looks fantastic but is very easy to prepare. Simply make the batter and prepare the fruit in advance, then combine the two and put in the oven at the start of the meal. It will be done just when you are ready to serve.

pear & fig clafoutis

3 ripe pears

3 ripe figs

¾ cup crème fraîche or sour cream

¾ cup milk

3 eggs

¾ cup sugar

2 tablespoons ground almonds

½ teaspoon ground cinnamon

confectioners' sugar, to dust

chilled light cream, to serve

a large, shallow ovenproof dish, well buttered

serves 4–6

Preheat the oven to 400ºF.

Peel and core the pears and cut into quite large pieces. Trim the stem ends from the figs and cut into slightly smaller pieces. If there is too much white on the fig skins, trim this off. Arrange the fruit in the prepared baking dish, distributing it evenly. Set aside.

Combine the crème fraîche, milk, eggs, sugar, almonds, and cinnamon in a large mixing bowl and beat well to combine.

Pour the batter evenly over the fruit and bake in the preheated oven for about 35–45 minutes, until puffed and golden. Let cool slightly and dust with confectioners' sugar just before serving. Serve warm with cream.

The word slump perfectly describes the sloppy batter which covers the seasonal fruit in this satisfying dessert. Normally the fruit is on the bottom and the thick batter spooned or poured roughly over the top but if you like to see more fruit, pour the batter in first, then push in the fruit and it works very well. You can use any juicy fruits and berries are really good too. Pine nuts can be substituted for the almonds if liked—simply sprinkle them all over the batter.

apricot & almond slump

Preheat the oven to 375°F.

Halve the apricots, remove the pits and mix with ½ cup of the sugar. Set aside until needed.

Sift the flour, baking powder, salt, and remaining sugar into a bowl. Stir in the ground almonds, the milk, and melted butter and whisk until smooth and thick. Pour the batter into the prepared pan, then push in the apricots cut-side up but in a higgledy-piggledy manner and slightly at an angle all over. Place a whole almond inside each apricot where the pit once was.

Bake in the preheated oven for 25–30 minutes, until risen and golden. Let cool slightly before serving with vanilla ice cream.

1 lb. 6 oz. apricots

¾ cup light soft brown sugar

¼ cup whole blanched almonds

vanilla ice cream, to serve

for the almond slump batter:

1½ cups all-purpose flour

3 teaspoons baking powder

a pinch of salt

1 cup ground almonds

scant 1½ cups milk

4 tablespoons unsalted butter, melted

a large, non-stick baking pan

serves 4–6

This is a homey dish, easy to make and even easier to eat. Pears make a nice change from apples, which are more commonly used in rustic home-baked desserts. If you prefer to use apples, choose a tart green apple and replace the grated orange peel with lemon.

pear slump

1½ lbs. pears, peeled, cored and sliced

½ cup light soft brown sugar

2 tablespoons all-purpose flour

1 teaspoon vanilla extract

finely grated peel of 1 orange

vanilla ice cream or whipped cream, to serve

for the slump batter:

2 cups all-purpose flour

1 cup sugar

1 tablespoon baking powder

a pinch of salt

1 cup milk

1 stick plus 1 tablespoon unsalted butter, melted

extra sugar or cinnamon sugar, to sprinkle

a large, shallow ovenproof dish, well-buttered

serves 4–6

Preheat the oven to 375°F.

In a bowl, combine the pears, sugar, flour, vanilla extract, and grated orange peel. Toss gently with your hands to combine and arrange in an even layer in the bottom of the prepared baking dish. Set aside.

To prepare the slump batter, combine the flour, sugar, baking powder, and salt in a separate bowl. In a third bowl or pitcher, stir together the milk and melted butter. Gradually pour the milk mixture into the dry ingredients, beating with a wooden spoon until just smooth.

Drop spoonfuls of the batter on top of the pears, leaving gaps but spreading to the edges. Sprinkle the top with sugar and bake in the preheated oven for 40–50 minutes, until golden brown. Serve warm with vanilla ice cream or whipped cream.

Granny Smith apples were first cultivated in Australia by Maria Ann Smith who saw their potential as a good all-round cooking apple. Their flesh collapses when cooked so they work well in this self-saucing dessert. Blueberries are used here but if you see mulberries (which are seasonal and rarely grown commercially), don't hesitate to use them in this recipe.

Granny Smith & blueberry pudding

Preheat the oven to 350°F.

Peel and core the apples then thinly slice them directly into the baking dish, arranging them in the bottom of the dish with the blueberries.

Sift the flour, baking powder, and sugar into a large bowl. Put the buttermilk and egg in a separate bowl. Use the tip of a small sharp knife to scrape the seeds from the vanilla bean directly into the buttermilk mixture. Pour this mixture into the flour mixture and beat well to combine.

Pour the batter over the fruit in the baking dish. Working quickly, put the brown sugar in a pitcher and add 1 cup boiling water. Stir until the sugar has dissolved. Carefully pour this mixture into the baking dish, pouring into a corner.

Bake in the preheated oven for 45 minutes, until the surface feels dry and springs back when lightly touched. Serve warm with cream.

2 tart green apples, such as Granny Smith

1 cup blueberries

1 cup all-purpose flour

3 teaspoons baking powder

½ cup plus 2 tablespoons sugar

1 cup buttermilk

1 egg

1 vanilla bean, split lengthwise

½ cup soft light brown sugar

chilled light cream, to serve

a large ovenproof dish, well buttered

serves 6

These soft, pear-shaped fruits have a sweet, honey-nectar flavor. Once picked, they ripen very quickly and late-season figs are perfect baked in desserts. This indulgent recipe is an excellent way to use up leftover stale croissants and can be put together in no time at all.

fig & honey croissant pudding

2 croissants, preferably stale, each torn into 6 pieces

6 figs, halved

¼ cup honey

3 eggs

1 cup milk

1 cup light cream

¼ cup sugar

chilled heavy cream, to serve

a medium ovenproof dish, lightly buttered

serves 4

Preheat the oven to 350°F.

Put the croissant pieces in the bottom of the prepared baking dish. Arrange the fig halves in between the croissant pieces and drizzle the honey over the top.

Combine the eggs, milk, cream, and sugar in a bowl and pour into the dish. Let sit for about 20 minutes to allow the croissants to absorb some of the liquid. Bake in the preheated oven for about 50 minutes, until the top of the pudding is a dark golden brown.

Let cool slightly before serving with heavy cream.

This is a very impressive dessert for relatively little work. The sweet and buttery brioche works well with the tangy blackberries. Try and find very sweet blackberries for this, as they will be softer and juicier, which is exactly what you want here. The dark purple juices should bleed into the brioche to create a pretty, marbled effect.

brioche pudding with blackberries

Preheat the oven to 350°F.

Slice the brioche to give you 6–8 thin slices. Lightly butter the slices on one side and arrange them in the bottom of a baking dish, overlapping them slightly. Arrange half of the blackberries on top. Repeat with the remaining brioche slices and blackberries.

Put the cream, eggs, milk, and sugar in a bowl or pitcher and beat to combine. Pour the mixture over the brioche in the baking dish. Cover with foil and let sit for 30 minutes to allow the brioche to absorb some of the liquid.

Sprinkle the demerara sugar over the top of the pudding and bake in the preheated oven for 40–45 minutes, until golden brown. Serve warm with vanilla ice cream.

4 brioche rolls (or half a 14-oz. brioche loaf)

½ stick unsalted butter, softened

2 cups blackberries

3 eggs

½ cup light cream

1½ cups milk

⅓ cup sugar

2 tablespoons demerara sugar

vanilla ice cream, to serve

a medium ovenproof dish

serves 6

This delightfully fresh-tasting pudding is based on a traditional British recipe. Served warm, the bottom layer forms a tangy, lemon sauce for the light sponge layer, but it is also delicious cold, when the sauce sets into a light custard that is lovely with the taste of blackberries. So there you are—two recipes for the price of one!

lemon & blackberry puddings

1 cup ripe blackberries

½ cup sugar, plus1 tablespoon

4 tablespoons unsalted butter, softened

1 vanilla bean, split lengthwise

grated peel and freshly squeezed juice of 1 large lemon

2 large eggs, separated

2 slightly heaping tablespoons all-purpose flour

1 cup milk

4 tablespoons light cream

½ teaspoon cream of tartar

chilled light cream, to serve

4–5 small ovenproof dishes, buttered

serves 4–5

Preheat the oven to 350°F.

Put the blackberries and the 1 tablespoon sugar in a bowl, toss gently, then spoon into the baking dishes.

Put the butter and the remaining sugar in a bowl and beat until creamy. Use the tip of a small sharp knife to scrape the vanilla seeds directly into the mixture and beat to mix. Beat in the grated lemon peel, followed by the egg yolks. Sift in the flour and fold in, then gradually beat in the milk, cream, and lemon juice.

Put the egg whites and cream of tartar in a separate, grease-free bowl and whisk until stiff but not dry. Beat 2 tablespoons of the egg whites into the mixture, then fold in the remainder with a spatula. Spoon the mixture into the prepared baking dishes. Put the dishes on a baking sheet and bake in the preheated oven for 30–35 minutes, until the sponge is golden. Serve hot or warm, with cream.

Variation To serve cold, bake in a 4-cup shallow ovenproof dish for an additional 5–10 minutes. Let cool (it will sink and deflate), then chill. When ready to serve, whisk 1 scant cup whipping cream and 2 tablespoons vanilla sugar in a bowl until billowy and thick. Spread the cream over the pudding, then decorate with extra blackberries and strips of lemon peel.

There is nothing better on a cold winter's day than the sound of a steamed pudding gently rattling in its pan. Smaller oranges are best here, and don't peel them—they are cooked, skins and all, for maximum effect. The dates keep the dark, sticky sponge beautifully moist.

chocolate, orange, & date steamed pudding

Submerge the orange slices in the sugar syrup. Set a disk of nonstick baking parchment on top and simmer gently for 30–40 minutes. Lift the oranges out with a slotted spoon and drain on a wire rack. Boil the syrup hard until reduced by half and set aside. Place the best orange slice on top of the paper disk in the pudding basin. Use the rest of the slices to line the sides.

In a large bowl, cream together the butter, muscovado sugar, and grated orange peel, until light and fluffy. Beat in the marmalade, then gradually beat in the eggs and orange flower water, if using, mixing very well between each addition. Sift the flour, cocoa, and baking powder onto a sheet of waxed paper, then fold into the egg mixture. Finally, fold in the dates.

Spoon the mixture into the orange-lined basin. Level the surface and cover with a disk of nonstick baking parchment. Take a large sheet of foil and fold it in half. Make a pleat in the center and place over the basin, with the pleat in the center. Press the foil over the side of the basin, tie around the top with string, and trim away any excess foil. Stand the basin on a trivet in a large, deep saucepan and add enough water to come at least 2 inches up the sides. Cover the pan with a lid and simmer gently for 2 hours, topping up the water level from time to time.

Remove the foil and paper disk and insert a skewer into the center of the pudding—if it doesn't come out clean, re-cover and steam for a little longer. Loosen the pudding around the sides with a knife, turn out onto a plate and brush with some of the reserved sugar syrup. Serve hot with crème anglaise.

2–3 seedless oranges, unpeeled and each one cut into 6 neat slices

⅔ cup sugar syrup*

1 stick plus 6 tablespoons unsalted butter, softened

1 cup dark muscovado sugar

finely grated peel of 1 unwaxed orange

3 tablespoons fine-cut orange marmalade

3 eggs, beaten

1 tablespoon orange flower water (optional)

1 cup plus 2 tablespoons all-purpose flour

6 tablespoons unsweetened cocoa powder

2 teaspoons baking powder

¾ cup pitted dates, chopped

hot crème anglaise, to serve

a 6-cup pudding basin, buttered and baselined with a disk of nonstick baking parchment

serves 6–8

* To make a simple sugar syrup, pour ⅔ cup water into a small saucepan and add ½ cup sugar. Cook over gentle heat until dissolved.

pies, tarts, & strudels

There are several different ways to top this alternative to a classic apple pie, including a lattice crust or this streusel topping, which is not strictly speaking Dutch as it actually comes from the Amish communities.

Dutch apple pie

Preheat the oven to 350°F.

Roll out the pastry on a floured work surface and line the pan with the pastry, all the way up the sides to the top edge. Let chill. Refrigerate while you prepare the apples.

Peel, core, and dice the apples and put them in a bowl. Add the sugar, golden raisins, cinnamon, and lemon juice and mix well using your hands.

In a food processor, combine all the topping ingredients, except the walnuts, and process to form coarse crumbs. Add the walnuts and pulse just a few times to combine.

Put the apple mixture in the pastry-lined pan. Sprinkle the streusel topping over the top in an even layer, going all the way to the edges and tidy up the edges of the pastry.

Cover with foil and bake in the preheated oven for about 30 minutes. Remove the foil and continue baking for a further 25–30 minutes, until the top of the pie is golden. Serve warm with whipped cream.

1 lb. 2 oz. ready-made shortcrust pastry, thawed if frozen

3 lbs. tart eating apples, such as Jonagold or Golden Delicious

½ cup sugar

¾ cup golden raisins

1 teaspoon ground cinnamon

1 tablespoon freshly squeezed lemon juice

whipped cream, to serve

for the streusel topping:

½ cup light soft brown sugar

½ cup less 2 tablespoons all-purpose flour

1 stick unsalted butter, chilled

1 teaspoon ground cinnamon

1 teaspoon ground nutmeg

1 teaspoon ground allspice

a pinch of salt

½ cup shelled walnuts, chopped

a springform cake pan, 9½ inches diameter, buttered and floured

serves 6—8

Apple pie afficionados believe that the best pies are made with a variety of apples to achieve a combination of sweet and tart flavors with both firm and melting textures.

classic apple pie

3 lbs. mixed apples, such Jonagold, Honey Crisp, and Golden Delicious, peeled and cored

¼ cup sugar, or more to taste

1 teaspoon ground cinnamon

1 tablespoon freshly squeezed lemon juice

chilled light cream, to serve

for the pie pastry:

2 cups plus 2 tablespoons all-purpose flour

1 teaspoon sugar

¼ teaspoon salt

⅔ stick unsalted butter

⅔ stick lard or vegetable shortening (such as Crisco)

1 egg yolk

1 egg, beaten

sugar, for sprinkling

a pie plate (with sloping sides), 9 inches diameter, buttered

serves 6–8

To make the pastry, put the flour, sugar, and salt in a food processor and process just to combine. Add the butter and lard and process using the pulse button until the mixture just forms coarse crumbs. Add the egg yolk and 4 tablespoons cold water and pulse again; the mixture should be crumbly but not holding together.

Transfer to a floured work surface and form into a ball. Cut in half, wrap well in plastic wrap, and chill for at least 1 hour. Roll out one dough half and use to line the bottom of the pie plate. Trim the edges leaving a ½ inch overhang and save the pastry trimmings for decoration. Chill while you prepare the apples.

Cut the apples into slices; not too thick and not too thin. Put them in a bowl with the sugar, cinnamon, and lemon juice and use your hands to mix well. Transfer to the lined pie plate.

Preheat the oven to 375°F.

Roll out the remaining dough on a floured work surface to a circle large enough to cover the apples. Brush the edges of the dough in the pie plate with beaten egg, then lay the other pastry circle on top. Fold over the overhang from the bottom layer and crimp using your fingertips, or use the tines of a fork to seal. Decorate as desired (a few leaves are traditional) and brush lightly with egg, then sprinkle with sugar. Cut 6–8 small slits in the top of the pie.

Put on a baking sheet and bake in the preheated oven for about 50–60 minutes, until golden. Serve warm with cream.

This twist on a classic recipe has a spice-filled pastry which takes on a golden color. Rolling out the rustic and crumbly pastry and filling it with lemon-infused apples is a very relaxing process you will want to enjoy again and again.

dusky apple pie

Put the apple slices in a large saucepan with the lemon juice, lemon peel, and sugar. Cover and cook over low heat for 15–20 minutes, turning the apples often so they soften and cook evenly. Set aside and let cool.

To make the pastry, put the flour, brown sugar, and spices in a food processor and process for a few seconds to combine. With the motor running, add the butter several cubes at a time. Add the egg and 1–2 tablespoons of cold water and process until combined. The dough will look dry and crumbly. Transfer to a bowl and knead to form a ball. Wrap the ball in plastic wrap and refrigerate for 30 minutes.

Preheat the oven to 350°F and put a baking sheet in the oven to heat up.

Cut the dough into two portions, with one slightly larger than the other. Roll out the larger piece of dough between two sheets of waxed paper and use it to line the bottom and sides of the prepared tart pan. Take care when handling the pastry as it will be quite crumbly.

Spoon the apples on top of the pastry base. Roll the remaining pastry to a circle large enough to cover the base and place on top of the pie, trimming the edges to fit. Use a small sharp knife to make several slits in the pastry. Put the pie on the hot baking sheet and bake in the preheated oven for 50–55 minutes, until the pastry is golden brown.

Remove the pie from the oven and let sit for 15–20 minutes before cutting into wedges and serving with vanilla ice cream.

8 tart green eating apples (such as Granny Smith), peeled, cored, and thinly sliced

2 teaspoons freshly squeezed lemon juice

2 thin slices of lemon peel

¼ cup sugar

2 cups self-rising flour

¾ cup light soft brown sugar

1 tablespoon ground cinnamon

1 tablespoon ground ginger

1 stick plus 1 tablespoon unsalted butter, chilled and cubed

1 egg, lightly beaten

vanilla ice cream, to serve

a loose-based fluted tart pan, 8 x 1½ inches high, lightly greased

serves 8–10

The method of using layers of buttered phyllo pastry and inverting the pie was inspired by the savory Moroccan pie called a "bastilla", but here the filling is vanilla-infused apples.

Moroccan apple pie

6 tart green eating apples, peeled, cored, and thinly sliced

1 teaspoon finely grated lemon peel

2 tablespoons freshly squeezed lemon juice

1 vanilla bean, split lengthwise

½ cup plus 2 tablespoons sugar

1 teaspoon ground cinnamon

1 teaspoon cornstarch

6 tablespoons unsalted butter, melted and cooled

8 sheets of phyllo pastry, thawed if frozen

confectioners' sugar, for dusting

chilled light cream, to serve

a springform cake pan, 9 inches diameter, lined with baking parchment

serves 8–10

Put the apples in a nonreactive bowl with the grated lemon peel and juice. Use the tip of a small sharp knife to scrape the vanilla seeds directly into the bowl with the apples. Add half of the sugar and toss to coat. Put the remaining sugar in a small bowl with the cinnamon and mix to combine. Set aside.

Put the apples in a saucepan with 2 tablespoons water and set over medium heat. Cover and cook for 10 minutes, stirring occasionally, until the apples are soft. Transfer the apples to a bowl and let cool. When completely cool, stir in the cornstarch.

Preheat the oven to 425°F. Put a baking sheet in the oven to heat. Brush the cake pan with a little melted butter.

Lay a sheet of phyllo on a clean work surface and lightly brush with melted butter. Sprinkle over some of the cinnamon sugar. Repeat using 3 more sheets of phyllo. Lift the phyllo into the cake pan. Gently press it into the pan, letting the ends hang over the rim. Repeat with the remaining phyllo, but lay the second stack across the first one so that the entire rim of the pan is draped in dough. Spoon the apples into the pan and use the back of a spoon to gently press them down. Fold the ends of the phyllo towards the center of the pan to enclose the filling. Lightly brush with melted butter.

Working quickly, remove the hot baking sheet from the oven and line with baking parchment. Carefully invert the pan onto the tray. Remove the side and base of the pan and brush the top of the pie with melted butter. Bake in the preheated oven for 30–35 minutes, until golden and crisp. Dust liberally with confectioners' sugar and serve warm with cream.

This appealingly sticky, fruity tart tastes better the day after it's made. Freezing the raspberries beforehand ensures that they keep their shape during baking and don't become too mushy.

raspberry & almond tart

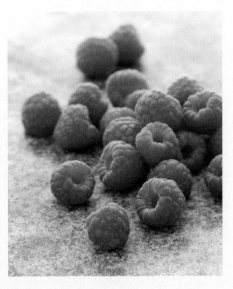

Preheat the oven to 350°F.

To make the pastry, put the ground almonds, flour, and sugar in a food processor. With the motor running, add a cube of butter at a time until it is all incorporated and the mixture resembles coarse bread crumbs. Add 2 tablespoons cold water and process until just combined. Do not overprocess.

Tip the dough out onto a lightly floured work surface and knead to form a ball. Roll the dough out between 2 layers of waxed paper until it is about 2 inches longer and 2 inches wider than the tart pan. Carefully lift the pastry into the pan and use your fingers to press it down into the base and sides, letting it overhang. Prick the base all over with a fork and bake in the preheated oven for 20 minutes, until lightly golden. Simply break off the overhanging pastry.

Put the egg, sugar, and flour in a bowl and whisk until thick and pale. Put the butter in a small saucepan and set over medium heat. Let melt until frothy and dark golden with a nutty aroma. Working quickly, pour the melted butter over the egg mixture and beat well. Scatter the frozen raspberries in the tart case. Pour the warm batter over the raspberries. Bake in the still-hot oven for about 45 minutes, until the top resembles a golden meringue. Let cool for 30 minutes before serving. Cut into slices and serve with cream.

6 oz. fresh raspberries, frozen until firm

1 egg

3 tablespoons sugar

1 tablespoon all-purpose flour

⅝ stick unsalted butter

chilled light cream, to serve

for the almond pastry:

⅓ cup ground almonds

1½ cups all-purpose flour

8 tablespoons sugar

1 stick unsalted butter, chilled and cubed

a rectangular tart pan, about 12 x 5 inches, lightly greased

serves 6—8

This deliciously easy recipe works best if the pears are on the overripe side so that they are fork-tender once cooked.

pear, almond, & mascarpone tart

4 very ripe pears

1 tablespoon freshly squeezed lemon juice

4 tablespoons sugar

½ cup mascarpone

1 egg

1 tablespoon all-purpose flour

⅔ cup slivered almonds

2 tablespoons sugar

chilled cream or vanilla ice cream, to serve

for the pastry:

1½ cups all-purpose flour

4 tablespoons sugar

4 tablespoons unsalted butter, chilled and cubed

a loose-bottomed tart pan, 10 inches diameter, lightly greased and floured

serves 8–10

To make the pastry, put the flour and sugar in a food processor and pulse to combine. With the motor running, add the butter and 1–2 tablespoons cold water and mix until the mixture resembles coarse bread crumbs and starts to gather in lumps. Transfer to a lightly floured surface and briefly knead to form a ball. Wrap in plastic wrap and chill for about 1 hour, until firm.

Preheat the oven to 350°F.

Coarsely grate the chilled pastry into a large bowl. Using lightly floured hands, scatter the grated pastry into the prepared tart pan and use your fingers to gently press it in, until the entire base and the side of the pan are covered. Bake in the preheated oven for about 25 minutes, until golden. Let cool.

Peel, halve, and core the pears. Put them in a nonreactive bowl with the lemon juice and 1 tablespoon of the sugar. Put the remaining sugar in a food processor. Add the mascarpone, egg, and flour and process to form a thick paste. Spread the mixture over the pastry. Arrange the pears on top, scatter over the almonds and sprinkle with sugar. Bake in the still-hot oven for 40–45 minutes, until the pears are soft and the mascarpone mixture has set. Slice and serve with cream or vanilla ice cream.

These individual tarts are so simple and quick to make. Use Red Delicious apples in early fall at a time when blueberries are in their last few weeks. Both fruits are perfect to cook with and lovely with vanilla. Any leftover tarts can be served cold with coffee the next day. Just dust them with some confectioners' sugar and eat them as you would a fruit-filled Danish.

apple & blueberry tarts

Preheat the oven to 425°F.

Lightly flour a work surface and unroll the pastry. Flatten it out and use a sharp knife or a pizza wheel to cut it into 4 squares. Transfer the squares to the prepared baking sheet.

Put the sugar and 2 tablespoons of water in a saucepan and bring to a boil, stirring until the sugar dissolves. Use the tip of a small sharp knife to scrape the vanilla seeds directly into the sugar syrup and stir to combine.

Add the apple slices to the pan, reduce the heat to medium, and cook for 4–5 minutes, turning the apples gently so they cook evenly. Add the blueberries and gently stir to coat them in the sweet syrup. Arrange the apples and blueberries on top of each pastry square. Bake in the preheated oven for 18–20 minutes, until the pastry is puffed and golden. Serve warm with the cream spooned over the top.

Variation For a simple French-style apple frangipane tart, mix 2 tablespoons each of softened butter, ground almonds, and confectioners' sugar with 1 tablespoon all-purpose flour in a bowl until you have a paste. Stir in 1 egg yolk until smooth. Spread the mixture over each of the pastry squares, leaving a space around the edge, and top with the apple slices. Bake in a preheated oven at 425°F for 18–20 minutes, until puffed and golden.

13-oz. sheet of ready-rolled puff pastry, thawed if frozen

2 tablespoons sugar

1 vanilla bean, split lengthwise

3 sweet eating apples, such as Red Delicious, cored and cut into wedges

1 cup blueberries

chilled heavy cream, to serve

a baking sheet lined with baking parchment

serves 4

You can use practically any fruit here; small peaches, nectarines, apricots, plums, apples, blueberries, pineapple, or a mixture of berries. Slivered almonds, walnuts, and pecans would also be good added to the fruits. To crush sugar cubes, put them in a plastic freezer bag and beat with the end of a rolling pin. Sprinkle over the tarts for a deliciously crunchy effect.

caramelized pear & cranberry tarts

13-oz. sheet of ready-rolled puff pastry, thawed if frozen

2 large ripe pears, peeled, halved and cored

1 oz. dried cranberries

2 tablespoons unsalted butter, chilled and cubed

milk, to glaze

3 tablespoons sugar or 2 oz. sugar cubes, crushed (see recipe introduction)

1 teaspoon ground cinnamon

chilled heavy cream or sour cream, to serve

serves 4

Preheat the oven to 425°F. Put a nonstick baking sheet in the oven to heat.

Lightly flour a work surface and unroll the pastry. Flatten it out and use a sharp knife or a pizza wheel to cut it into 4 squares.

Place a pear half in the center of each pastry square and divide the dried cranberries between the squares. Scatter with the diced butter. Brush the edges with a little milk. Mix the sugar or crushed sugar cubes with the cinnamon and sprinkle over the top.

Carefully slide the tarts onto the hot baking sheet and return to the preheated oven to cook for about 35–40 minutes, until the pastry is golden brown and crisp and the pears are tender. Serve warm with cream or sour cream.

Which apple variety to use for a tarte tatin is the source of much debate. Golden Delicious are good because they hold their shape well and the mild flavor complements the rich caramel.

tarte tatin

To make the pastry, put the flour, sugar, butter, and salt in a food processor and using the pulse button, process until the mixture is just combined (about 5–10 pulses). Add 3–4 tablespoons cold water and pulse just until the dough holds together. Wrap the dough in waxed paper and let stand in a cool place for 30–60 minutes before rolling out.

Roll out the pastry on a floured work surface. Turn the tart pan upside-down on the rolled out dough and trace around it with the tip of a sharp knife. Transfer to a large plate and chill.

Put the butter and sugar in the tart pan and set over high heat. Melt, stirring to blend. Remove from the heat and arrange the apple quarters in the pan in 2 circles. (The inner circle should go in the opposite direction to the outer circle.) Return to the heat and cook for about 30 minutes. From this point, watch the apples carefully and cook for a further 5–15 minutes, until the liquid thickens and caramelizes.

Preheat the oven to 400°F. Remove the pan from the heat and top with the pastry round, gently tucking in the edges. Transfer to the preheated oven and bake for about 45 minutes, until browned. Let cool only slightly. Carefully invert the tart onto a serving plate so that the pastry is on the bottom. Serve at room temperature with crème fraîche or sour cream.

1 stick plus 2 tablespoons unsalted butter

¾ cup sugar

3 lbs. tart eating apples, such as Golden Delicious or Cox's, peeled, cored, and quartered

crème fraîche or sour cream, to serve

for the sweet pastry dough:

1½ cups all-purpose flour

2 teaspoons sugar

1 stick less 1 tablespoon unsalted butter, chilled and cubed

a heavy, flameproof tàrte tatin pan (ideally enamelled cast iron or lined copper), about 10 inches diameter

serves 6

What could be better than the simplicity of pears poached in red wine? This tart is! The fruit absorbs the deep flavor of the wine and turn a fabulously rich color. If you want to be outrageously extravagant, use Italian Vin Santo or Marsala instead of the wine and reduce the quantity of sugar—the pears will be a beautiful dark mahogany.

drunken pear tart

8 under-ripe medium pears

1 cinnamon stick

⅓ cup sugar

2¾ cups full-bodied red wine

slivered pistachios or almonds, to finish

crème fraîche or sour cream, to serve

for the pâte brisée:

1½ cups all-purpose flour

a large pinch of salt

1 stick unsalted butter, diced, at room temperature

1 egg yolk

2½–3 tablespoons ice water

a cast-iron skillet, 10 inches diameter

serves 6

To make the pastry, sift the flour and salt into a mound on a clean work surface. Make a well in the center with your fist. Put the butter and egg yolk into the well and using the fingers of one hand "peck" the eggs and butter together until they resemble scrambled eggs. Using a palette knife, flick the flour over the egg mixture and chop through until almost amalgamated. Sprinkle with the water and chop again. Bring together quickly with your hands. Knead lightly into a ball, then flatten slightly. Wrap in plastic wrap and chill for at least 30 minutes. Let return to room temperature before rolling out.

Peel the pears, halve lengthwise and carefully scoop out the core with a teaspoon or melon baller. Arrange them around the base of the skillet in concentric circles. Crumble the cinnamon over the top and sprinkle with the sugar. Pour in the red wine, bring to a boil, then cover and simmer gently for about 1 hour, until tender.

Preheat the oven to 400°F. Uncover the pan and hold the pan lid over the pears to hold them back while you pour off the juices into a saucepan. Boil the juices until well reduced and syrupy, then pour back over the pears.

Roll out the dough on a lightly floured work surface to a circle slightly larger than the pan. Lift the pastry over the pears and tuck the edge of the pastry down into the pan. Bake for 35–40 minutes, until the pastry is crisp and golden. As soon as it is ready, invert the tart onto a plate, sprinkle with nuts and serve warm with crème fraîche or sour cream.

Versions of this tart are sold at pâtisseries all over France. When peaches are in season and at their best, they appear in the window in all their rustic glory. So simple to make and so good to eat! If you want to use ready-made puff pastry, that's fine, but you should try this easy cheat's recipe at least once.

free-form peach tart

To make the pastry, sift the flour and salt into a large bowl. Hold the frozen butter in a kitchen towel and, using the large side of a box grater, quickly grate the butter into the flour. Stir the butter into the flour with a palette knife until it is evenly distributed. Sprinkle the water over the surface, then mix with the knife until the dough starts to come together in a messy lump. Tip this onto a floured work surface and knead lightly until it forms a streaky, lumpy ball. Flatten the ball with the palm of your hand. Wrap in plastic wrap and chill for about 30 minutes until firm. Roll out away from you into a rectangle 3 times longer than it is wide—no exact measurements are needed here but it should be about ¼ inch thick. Lightly mark the pastry into 3 equal sections with a blunt knife. Fold the third closest to you up over the middle third, then bring the top third towards you over the folded two-thirds. Rewrap and chill for 15 minutes. Repeat twice more. Wrap and chill for 30 minutes.

Preheat the oven to 450°F. Roll out the pastry on a lightly floured work surface and cut out a circle using a large dinner plate as a template. Lift onto a baking sheet and make an edge by twisting the pastry over itself all the way around the edge. Press lightly to seal. Still on the baking sheet, chill or freeze for 30 minutes.

Peel the peaches, then halve and pit them and cut into chunky slices. Put the butter into a large saucepan, then add the lemon juice and half the sugar. Heat until melted, then add the peaches and toss gently. Pile the peaches over the pastry. Sprinkle with the remaining sugar and bake in the preheated oven for 20–25 minutes, until golden, puffed and caramelized. Serve with whipped cream or sour cream.

4–6 ripe peaches

5 tablespoons butter

freshly squeezed juice of ½ a lemon

1 cup sugar

whipped cream or sour cream, to serve

for the cheat's puff pastry:

2 cups all-purpose flour

a pinch of salt

1½ sticks unsalted butter, frozen

about ½ cup ice water

a dinner plate, about 12 inches diameter (to use as a template)

serves 6

These unusual tartlets are a cheese course and dessert rolled into one making them a fabulous finale for any dinner party.

pear, gorgonzola, & pecan tartlets

13-oz. sheet of ready-rolled puff pastry, thawed if frozen

1 egg, lightly beaten

7 oz. Gorgonzola

4 tablespoons heavy cream

2–3 ripe pears

½ cup pecan halves

6 teaspoons pure maple syrup

cayenne pepper, to taste

serves 6

Preheat the oven to 425°F.

Unroll the pastry, cut it in half horizontally, then cut each of the halves into 3 to make 6 equal-sized pieces. With the tip of a sharp knife, score round each of the squares about ½ inch from the edge to make a border. Lightly brush the border with beaten egg, taking care not to brush over the cut you've made (otherwise the pastry won't puff up around the edge of the tartlets).

Put the Gorgonzola in a bowl and break up roughly with a fork, then stir in the cream. Season with a little cayenne pepper and spread over the bases of the tartlets, taking care not to cover the border. Roughly break up the pecan nuts and divide between the tartlets. Peel, core, and quarter the pears, cut each quarter into 3 wedges and lay them in slices on top of the cheese and nuts. Drizzle a teaspoonful of maple syrup over each tart and bake in the preheated oven for 15–20 minutes, until the pastry is well browned and puffed up. Let cool for 5 minutes before serving.

Apple tart is a classic but this recipe represents a slight departure. The combination of apples and vanilla is absolutely divine so a layer of vanilla-scented apple purée has been added.

apple tart

Roll out the pastry dough on a floured work surface to a circle slightly larger than the prepared tart pan. Transfer the dough to the pan. To trim the edges, roll a rolling pin over the top, using the edge of the pan as a cutting surface, letting the excess pastry fall away. Refrigerate for 30 minutes, until firm.

To bake blind, preheat the oven to 400°F. Prick the pastry base all over, line with baking parchment and fill with baking weights. Bake in the preheated oven for 15 minutes, then remove the paper and weights and bake for a further 10–15 minutes, until golden. Let cool before filling.

To make the apple and vanilla purée, put the apples, vanilla bean, sugar, and butter in a saucepan with 3–4 tablespoons water. Cook gently, stirring often, for about 10–15 minutes until soft (adding more water if necessary). Remove the vanilla bean, use the tip of a small sharp knife to scrape the vanilla seeds directly into the mixture, then discard the bean. Transfer the mixture to a food processor and purée until smooth.

Preheat the oven to 375°F. Spread the purée evenly in the pastry case. Arrange the apple slices in a neat circle around the edge; they should be slightly overlapping. Repeat to create an inner circle, trimming the slices slightly so that they fit, going in the opposite direction from the outer circle. Brush with melted butter and sprinkle over the sugar.

Bake in the preheated oven for 25–25 minutes, until the apples are just browned and tender. Serve warm with cream.

1 quantity Sweet Pastry Dough (see page 117), at room temperature

3 mild eating apples, such as Golden Delicious, peeled, cored, and sliced

1 tablespoon unsalted butter, melted

1 tablespoon sugar

chilled light cream, to serve

For the apple and vanilla purée

3 apples (any variety), peeled, cored, and diced

1 vanilla bean, split lengthwise

2–4 tablespoons sugar, to taste

2 teaspoons unsalted butter

a loose-based tart pan, 10 inches diameter, buttered and lightly floured

serves 6–8

This is a classic French pastry. Sometimes the pears are simply halved, but it looks more attractive if they are sliced.

pear & almond tart

1 part-baked sweet pastry case, 10 inches diameter or 14 x 4½ inches, as shown (see Sweet Pastry Dough, page 117 and baking blind method, page 125)

1 stick less 1 tablespoon unsalted butter, softened

½ cup sugar

2 large eggs

⅔ cup ground almonds

2 tablespoons all-purpose flour

seeds from ½ a vanilla bean split lengthwise, or 1 teaspoon vanilla extract

3–4 ripe pears, such as Williams, peeled, cored, and sliced

vanilla ice cream or hot crème anglaise, to serve

serves 6

Preheat the oven to 375°F.

In a mixing bowl, combine the butter and sugar and beat until light and fluffy. Add the eggs one at a time, beating well with each addition. Add the almonds, flour, and vanilla seeds and mix just to combine.

Spoon the almond mixture into the pastry case and level the surface. Arrange the pear slices on top.

Bake in the preheated oven for 20–25 minutes, until puffed and golden. Serve warm with ice cream or crème anglaise.

Fresh ricotta cheese is combined here with summer-ripe cherries and crispy phyllo pastry with great success. Best of all, you can make this in advance and freeze it. There is no need to thaw before cooking—just give it a little more time in the oven. You could also try using sliced green apples instead of the cherries.

cherry & ricotta strudel

Put the cherries, 1 tablespoon of the confectioners' sugar, and the cornstarch in a bowl. Stir and let sit for 30 minutes

Preheat the oven to 425°F. Put a baking sheet in the oven to heat up.

Put the ground almonds and 2 tablespoons of the remaining confectioners' sugar in a bowl and mix to combine. Put the ricotta in a separate bowl, add the remaining confectioners' sugar, and mix to combine. Set aside until needed.

Put a sheet of baking parchment on a work surface. Lay a sheet of phyllo on the baking parchment, longest edge nearest to you. Brush all over with melted butter until the phyllo is shiny. Sprinkle 1–2 tablespoons of the ground almond mixture over the pastry. Repeat with the remaining sheets of phyllo, melted butter, and almond mixture, finishing with the final sheet of phyllo.

Working quickly, so that the phyllo does not become soggy, spread the ricotta mixture over the pastry, leaving a 2-inch margin around the edges. Spoon the cherry mixture over the top. Fold the edge nearest to you up and over the filling, tucking in the shorter edges as you roll. Make sure the strudel is sitting seam-side down. Use the baking parchment to lift the strudel onto the hot baking sheet. Bake in the preheated oven for 12–15 minutes, until lightly golden brown. Remove and let cool slightly before dusting liberally with confectioners' sugar and cutting into slices to serve.

1 lb. cherries, pitted and halved

⅓ cup confectioners' sugar, plus extra for dusting

2 teaspoons cornstarch

8 sheets of phyllo pastry, thawed if frozen

⅔ cup ground almonds

6 oz. fresh ricotta

5 tablespoons unsalted butter, melted

serves 8

Praline powder is a great "secret" ingredient. It's a cinch to prepare and makes a great addition to many desserts. Here it teams up with crispy phyllo pastry to lift what would be an ordinary strudel well above the average.

praline apple strudel

1 lb. tart eating apples, such as Cox's Orange Pippin, peeled, cored, and chopped

¼ cup mixed dried fruit, such as golden raisins, cranberries, or sour cherries

½ cup light soft brown sugar

1 teaspoon ground cinnamon

1 tablespoon unsalted butter

6 sheets phyllo pastry, thawed if frozen

½ stick unsalted butter, melted

confectioners' sugar, to dust

whipped cream or sour cream, to serve

for the praline:

½ cup pecan halves

¼ cup sugar

a baking sheet lined with baking parchment

serves 6–8

To make the praline, combine the pecans and sugar in a nonstick heavy-based skillet and cook over medium/high heat, stirring constantly, until the sugar hardens and coats the nuts. Transfer to a plate to cool, then process in a coffee grinder or food processor until ground to a coarse powder. Set aside.

In a large saucepan, combine the apples, dried fruit, brown sugar, cinnamon, and 1 tablespoon butter. Cook over medium heat for about 15 minutes, until the apples are soft and the juices have evaporated. Remove from the heat and let cool.

Preheat the oven to 375°F.

Put 2 sheets of phyllo on the prepared baking sheet and brush with some melted butter. Sprinkle with a little praline. Top with 2 more sheets of phyllo and repeat. Top with 2 more sheets of phyllo. Spread the apple mixture in an even layer over the top sheet of phyllo. Sprinkle with more praline mixture, then carefully roll up from a long end, as you would a jelly roll. Use the baking parchment to help you roll, if necessary. Make sure the strudel is sitting seam-side down. Brush with a little more melted butter and sprinkle with any remaining praline. Bake in the preheated oven for 25–35 minutes, until crisp and golden.

Let cool slightly before dusting with confectioners' sugar. Serve warm with whipped cream or sour cream.

This simple recipe can be made with whatever fruit is in season, such as apples, pears, or apricots—but plums are probably the nicest. How you shape the pastries depends upon the way the puff pastry dough is packaged: squares, circles, and triangles all work fine. Be sure to use just-soft plums, not too ripe.

baked plums in puff pastry

Preheat the oven to 375°F.

Roll out the pastry on a floured surface to make 4 rectangles, each about 6 x 3½ inches. Arrange the pastry squares on the prepared baking sheet. Brush with the egg and sprinkle each rectangle very generously with about 4 tablespoons of the sugar. Bake in the preheated oven for 15–20 minutes, until puffed and browned. Remove from the oven and let cool. Do not turn the oven off.

Cut the plums in half, remove the pits, then slice each half into quarters. Put the plums in a baking dish, sprinkle with the remaining sugar and bake in the still-hot oven for about 20–30 minutes, until tender and slightly browned. Let cool.

To assemble, split the pastries in half with a sharp knife, but not all the way through. Fill with a generous dollop the sweetened sour cream and plums. Serve immediately, while the pastry is still crisp.

13-oz. sheet of ready-rolled puff pastry, thawed if frozen

1 egg, beaten

about 4 tablespoons caster sugar

6–8 large red plums (not too ripe)

scant ¾ cup sugar

1 cup sour cream, sweetened to taste with sugar

a baking sheet lined with baking parchment

serves 4

dessert cakes

Sweet summer strawberries are baked in a smooth, dense cake given a light and creamy crumb by using buttermilk. It can be made in a conventional round cake pan or baked in a square pan and cut into squares to serve (like a brownie). Small strawberries are fine left whole but do halve or quarter large ones before folding them through the batter.

strawberry buttermilk cake

Preheat the oven to 350°F.

Put the flour and sugar in a bowl and stir to mix. Put the butter, eggs, and buttermilk in the bowl of a food processor and process until smooth and combined. With the motor running, add the flour and sugar and process until well mixed. Scrape down the sides of the bowl to evenly incorporate all the ingredients. Transfer to a mixing bowl and stir in the strawberries. Spoon the mixture into the prepared cake pan and level the top.

To make the topping, put the flour and butter in a bowl and, using your fingertips, rub the butter into the flour until the mixture resembles coarse bread crumbs. Stir in the sugar.

Sprinkle the topping mixture evenly over the cake mixture. Bake in the preheated oven for 50 minutes, until the top is golden brown.

Let cool before cutting into squares and serving with crème anglaise or cream.

2 cups self-rising flour

1 cup plus 2 tablespoons sugar

1 stick unsalted butter, softened

2 eggs

1 cup buttermilk

13 oz. strawberries, hulled

hot crème anglaise or chilled heavy cream, to serve

for the topping:

5 tablespoons all-purpose flour

½ stick unsalted butter, chilled and cubed

½ cup light soft brown sugar

a cake pan, 8 inches square, greased and baselined

serves 6—8

Somewhere between a shortcake and a scone, this cake has all the hallmarks of a great recipe. It's easy, delicious, and has the "I can't believe I made this myself" factor. Because the method is so simple the final result is largely dependent on the quality of the fruit used, so do choose the best peaches, still firm with that heady peach fragrance.

peach & raspberry scone cake

½ cup good-quality raspberry preserve

1 cup whipping cream, whipped

2 fresh peaches, pitted and sliced

2 cups raspberries

for the scone cake:

2¾ cups self-rising flour

1 cup light cream

1 cup clear, sparkling lemonade (not low calorie or reduced sugar)

a fluted, loose-bottomed tart pan, about 8 inches diameter, lightly greased

serves 8

Preheat the oven to 350°F) Gas 4.

Put the flour in a large bowl and make a well in the center. Add the cream and lemonade and use a wooden spoon to mix together.

Spoon the mixture into the prepared pan, gently pressing down to fit. Bake in the preheated oven for 30–35 minutes, until golden brown on top. Let cool.

Using a long, sharp knife, slice about ¼ inch off the top of the cake to create a level surface. Spread the preserve evenly over the top of the cake.

Spoon the whipped cream on top of the cake, arrange the peaches slices and raspberries on top and serve immediately.

This is a deliciously spicy cake with a very moreish texture. Ground ginger loses its intensity if left sitting in the kitchen cupboard for too long, so do make sure that what you use here is still fragrant. You can make this recipe substituting apples for the pears. If you do decide to try it this way, use ground cinnamon instead of ginger.

pear & ginger crumble cake

Preheat the oven to 350°F.

To make the crumble mixture, put the flour and ginger in a large bowl. Add the butter and quickly rub it into the flour using your fingertips. Add the sugar and rub again until the mixture resembles coarse sand. Refrigerate until needed.

Beat the butter and sugar until pale and creamy. Add the eggs, one at a time, and beat well between each addition. Tip in the flour and baking powder and beat for 1 minute, until the mixture is smooth and well combined. Pour it into the prepared cake pan. Toss the pears in a bowl with the lemon juice and put them on top of the cake. Sprinkle the crumble topping over the top. Bake in the preheated oven for 40–45 minutes, until golden on top.

Let cool slightly before removing from the pan and serve warm with cream.

1 stick unsalted butter, softened

½ cup plus 2 tablespoons sugar

2 eggs, at room temperature

1 cup all-purpose flour

2 teaspoons baking powder

2 firm pears, peeled, cored, and sliced

1 tablespoon freshly squeezed lemon juice

chilled heavy cream, to serve

for the ginger crumble:

½ cup all-purpose flour

1 teaspoon ground ginger

3 tablespoons soft light brown sugar

½ stick unsalted butter, chilled and cubed

a springform cake pan, 9 inches diameter, baselined and lightly greased

You can use either yellow or white peaches here. Yellow peaches have a more robust flavor whereas the white ones have a more subtle flavor that is more like that of nectarines, which are, after all, just peaches without the fuzzy skin!

upside-down peach cake

4 large peaches

1 stick unsalted butter, softened

1 scant cup light soft brown sugar

3 eggs, separated

¾ cup plus 2 tablespoons self-rising flour

1 cup sour cream

confectioners' sugar, for dusting

chilled light cream, to serve

a springform cake pan, 9 inches diameter, baselined and lightly greased

Preheat the oven to 350°F.

Halve the peaches, discard the pit, then cut each into quarters. Arrange the peaches on the bottom of the prepared cake pan and set aside.

Put the butter and sugar in a large bowl and beat until the sugar has completely dissolved and the mixture is the color of caramel. Add the egg yolks, one at a time, beating for 1 minute between each addition. Fold the flour and sour cream through in two batches.

In a separate grease-free bowl, beat the egg whites until they form firm peaks. Using a large metal spoon, fold the whites into the cake mixture in batches. Spoon the mixture over the peaches and level the surface. Bake in the preheated oven for 40–45 minutes, until the top of the cake is golden and the center springs back when gently pressed.

Let cool for 10 minutes in the pan before carefully turning out. Dust with confectioners' sugar and serve warm with cream.

This cake hails from Somerset, in England, but as traditional West Country cooking can be a little spartan, the basic recipe here has been jazzed up with some honey and spices.

spiced apple cake

Preheat the oven to 325°F.

Put the butter and brown sugar in a mixing bowl and cream together until light and fluffy. Beat in the honey. In a separate bowl, combine the flours, baking powder, cinnamon, cloves, ginger, and nutmeg.

Fold the dry ingredients into the butter mixture, then add the eggs and mix well. Fold in the ground almonds, golden raisins, apples, and milk and mix just to combine. Transfer the mixture to the prepared pan and level the top.

Bake in the preheated oven for 50–60 minutes, until risen and golden and a skewer inserted in the center of the cake comes out clean. Let cool slightly in the pan then turn out onto a wire rack. When cool, sprinkle with slivered almonds and dust with confectioners' sugar. Cut into squares to serve.

2 sticks unsalted butter, softened

1 cup light soft brown sugar

6 tablespoons honey

2 cups whole-wheat flour

⅔ cup all-purpose flour

2 teaspoons baking powder

1 teaspoon ground cinnamon

½ teaspoon ground cloves

½ teaspoon ground ginger

½ teaspoon ground nutmeg

5 eggs, beaten

3 tablespoons ground almonds

½ cup golden raisins

1 lb. 4 oz. tart cooking apples, peeled, cored, and finely chopped

4 tablespoons milk

3–4 tablespoons slivered almonds, toasted

confectioners' sugar, for dusting

a cake pan, 9 inches square, buttered and lightly floured

makes 16 squares

Use sweet eating apples here as they keep their shape, unlike cooking apples which can result in a wet and mushy cake. If you are using the standard size of ramekin this recipe will serve six, but if you have the larger ones it will serve four. The cakes can be cooked ahead of time, but leave them in the dishes and reheat in a warm oven before turning out and serving.

upside-down apple cakes

1 stick plus 4 tablespoons unsalted butter, plus extra for greasing

½ cup light soft brown sugar

12 oz. sweet eating apples, peeled, cored, and roughly chopped

finely grated peel of ½ a lemon

½ teaspoon ground nutmeg

½ teaspoon ground cinnamon

1 oz. walnut halves, chopped

½ cup plus 1 tablespoon sugar

1 scant cup self-rising flour

1 teaspoon baking powder

2 eggs

for the ginger cream:

¼ cup crème fraîche or sour cream

2 pieces of stem ginger in syrup, drained and finely chopped

1 teaspoon of syrup from the stem ginger

6 x ½-cup or 4 x 1-cup ramekins, lightly greased

serves 4–6

Preheat the oven to 350°F.

Put the brown sugar and 4 tablespoons of the butter in a heavy-based saucepan with 2 tablespoons water and heat until melted. Gradually bring to a boil and cook for about 1 minute, or until caramelized. Spoon 1 tablespoon of the caramel sauce into the base of each prepared ramekin. Set aside the remaining sauce.

Put the apples, grated lemon peel, nutmeg, cinnamon, and walnuts in a large bowl and mix to combine. Divide the mixture between the ramekins.

To make the sponge, put the remaining butter, sugar, flour, and baking powder in the bowl of a food processor and blend for a couple of seconds before adding the eggs. Process for a further 10–15 seconds, then stop as soon as the mixture comes together. Spoon the cake batter into the ramekins. Place them on a baking sheet and cook in the preheated oven for 15–20 minutes, until the sponge bounces back when lightly touched.

Meanwhile, to make the ginger cream, mix together the crème fraîche, stem ginger, and ginger syrup. Remove the cakes from the oven and run a knife around the edges. Leave to sit for about 5 minutes before inverting onto serving plates. To serve, reheat the reserved caramel sauce and spoon it over the cakes. Serve topped with a spoonful of the ginger cream.

If you can get hold of blood oranges they are the best ones to use here. They have a sherberty flavor with hints of raspberry and a divine color. The fact that they are a truly seasonal fruit, available only for a few months in the year, makes them even more special.

almond & orange syrup cake

Preheat the oven to 350°F.

Put the almonds in a food processor and process until finely chopped. Transfer to a bowl and mix in the sugar and flour.

Beat the butter and grated orange peel for 1 minute, then add the eggs, one at a time, beating well after each addition until well mixed. Add the almond mixture in two batches and beat again until well combined. Spoon into the prepared cake pan. Bake in the preheated oven for 45 minutes, until golden on top. Remove the cake from the oven and prick it all over with a toothpick or skewer.

To make the syrup, put the orange juice and sugar in a small saucepan and set over high heat. Stir until the sugar has dissolved. As soon as the mixture boils remove the pan from the heat and pour the syrup over the cake.

Let the cake cool in the pan then sprinkle the slivered almonds on top. Slice and serve with cream.

1½ cups blanched almonds

1 cup plus 2 tablespoons sugar

6 tablespoons self-rising flour

2 sticks unsalted butter, softened

1 tablespoon finely grated orange peel

4 eggs

½ cup slivered almonds, lightly toasted

extra thick heavy cream, to serve

for the orange syrup:

¼ cup freshly squeezed orange juice

¼ cup sugar

a springform cake pan, 9 inches diameter, lightly greased

serves 8

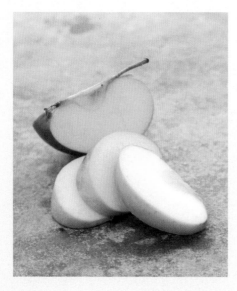

The whisked sponge method of cake making is popular in Italy and this recipe from Tuscany is very light in texture and studded with juicy chunks of apple. You can change the spice to cinnamon if you prefer but use a little more, as it is not as assertive as cloves. Italian cooks sometimes add finely chopped fresh rosemary to theirs, which makes it taste very special.

apple & lemon sponge cake

1 stick unsalted butter

4 sweet eating apples

finely grated peel of 2 lemons and the freshly squeezed juice of ½ a lemon

¼ teaspoon ground cloves

4 eggs

¾ cup sugar

¾ cup all-purpose flour

1 teaspoon baking powder

a pinch of salt

3 tablespoons apricot preserve, melted

a springform cake pan, 9 inches diameter, well buttered and baselined

serves 8

Melt the butter in a saucepan, then set aside to cool. Peel, core, and cut the apples into medium chunks and put them in a bowl. Add the grated lemon peel, cloves, and juice and toss to coat.

Put the eggs and sugar in a heatproof bowl and set it over a saucepan of simmering water. Whisk for about 15 minutes until glossy, thick, and pale and doubled in volume. The mixture should hold a trail when the whisk is lifted out of the bowl. Remove the bowl from the heat and continue whisking for a further 5–10 minutes, until the mixture is cool.

Preheat the oven to 350°F.

Sift the flour, baking powder, and salt together into a large bowl. Gently fold half the flour into the whisked mixture. Pour the cooled melted butter around the edge of the mixture and fold in. Fold in the remaining flour, then two-thirds of the apples. Be very careful when folding in—you want to keep as much air in the mixture as possible. Spoon the remaining apples into the base of the pan, then pour the cake mixture over the apples. Bake in the preheated oven for about 40 minutes, until risen, golden brown, and firm when gently pressed in the center.

Let cool in the pan for 5 minutes before inverting onto a wire rack to cool. Brush the top with the melted apricot preserve just before serving.